NOTHING TO LOSE 2

**DOMINGO 10:00 AM
CENTRO DE AYUDA**

68-03 ROOSEVELT AVE. (ESQ. CON LA CALLE 69)
WOODSIDE, QUEENS NY 11377
S.O.S LÍNEA DE AYUDA: (718) 458-3415

Edir Macedo

NOTHING TO LOSE 2

MY CHALLENGES
WHEN FACING THE
IMPOSSIBLE

 Planeta

Work published in collaboration with Editora Planeta do Brasil Ltda – Brasil

Copyright © Edir Macedo, 2013

Original Title: Nada a perder 2. Meus desafios diante do impossível

Original Publisher: Editorial Planeta Do Brasil Ltda., 2013

Translation: Derek Sevante
Copyediting: Fernanda Umile
Proofreading: Lizete Mercadante Machado
Graphic Project: Thiago Sousa | all4type.com.br
Designing: Max Oliveira
Cover: Repertório Editorial
Cover Image: Demétrio Koch
Core Photos: Arquivo Diário de São Paulo, Archivo Jornal do Brasil, Baboon Filmes, Lumi Zúnica, Demétrio Koch, José Célio, Pauty Araújo, Ticiana Bitencourt, Marcos A. Silva, Kátia Pedroza, Lucas Prado, Arlesson Sicsú, Luciana Botelho, Getty images/Mike Theiss, archive personal, Reprodução TV Record and Cedoc/Unipro
Collaboration: Karla Dunder, Marcus Souza, Anne Campos, Vagner Silva y Leandro Cipoloni
Acknowledgements: Clodomir Santos, Paulo Roberto Guimarães, Cristiane Cardoso, Renato Cardoso, Viviane Freitas, Júlio Freitas, Marcus Vinicius Vieira, Romualdo Panceiro, Guaracy Santos, Honorilton Gonçalves, Sérgio Corrêa, Sérgio Motta, Tânia Maduro, Solange Guimarães, Marcos Pereira, Adriana Guerra, Ivone de Paula, Rita Cruz, Terezinha Rosa Silva, Mariléa Sales, Alba Maria and Sheila Tavolaro

© 2014, Editorial Planeta Mexicana, S.A. de C.V.
Bajo el sello editorial PLANETA M.R.
Avenida Presidente Masarik núm. 111, 2o. piso
Colonia Chapultepec Morales
C.P. 11570, México, D.F.
www.editorialplaneta.com.mx

First edition in English: February of 2014
ISBN: 978-607-07-2037-6

Impreso en los talleres de Litográfica Ingramex, S.A. de C.V.
Centeno núm. 162-1, colonia Granjas Esmeralda, México, D.F.
Impreso en México – *Printed in Mexico*

To God, the Holy Spirit, who in the name of His Son Jesus, has guided my life.

To Ester, my beloved and faithful companion.

CONTENTS

INTRODUCTION

I confess that when I decided to record my memories, I imagined putting together a limited biographical project. I never imagined that the demand for *Nothing to Lose* would grow so rapidly to such startling proportions.

The scenes of the release of the first book in this trilogy, which attracted huge crowds in Brazil and all over the world, moved me and filled me with such joy and gratitude. Gratitude for the faithful people who have followed our journey of surrender on the altar, and gratitude above all, to the Holy Spirit for all He has done, is doing and will do in our lives.

It also taught me more about the designs of God. Many situations that my wife Ester and I have lived through, which we did not understand at the time, today serve as a compass for countless people today. We were unaware that the Spirit of God guided us in those moments so our life story could strengthen, encourage, instruct, renew and inspire in both small and big ways, and save people of all languages, races, cultures and continents.

There were forty-six official releases of *Nothing to Lose 1* worldwide: four continents, sixteen countries, and forty-one cities. Close to one million came to bookstores from New York to Rio de Janeiro, from Tokyo to London, from Paris to Caracas, from Manila to Johannesburg, and from Hong Kong to Manaus. During the cycle of releases, the book was given to officials of the United Nations in the US, and to many media outlets worldwide. Remote tribes in Africa and prison inmates of São Paulo—where I made a point to appear personally to shake hands and pray for each one—showed the same degree of respect and admiration for the book. It was an honor for me.

This project broke records and won over the most varied audiences in various corners of the world. But no amount of positive feedback can give me a greater sense of reward and satisfaction than the thousands of testimonies of readers who have been helped by *Nothing to Lose 1*. Offering a light at the end of the tunnel for those who feel lost, sharing my personal experience with the Almighty and helping others are the main goals of this project.

Now we launch into the second part of this trilogy of faith. Find out how everything happened in Brazil. Discover what is possible through the Word of God. How a tiny church in a small funeral home spread into thousands of churches; from meetings in the neighborhood of Abolição, in Rio de Janeiro, to preaching in large soccer stadiums and the largest fairgrounds of the country. The painful path to acquire ownership of Record TV Network, which today is one of the top TV networks in Brazil and the world.

Intensive journalistic research helped create a solid base for my memories and thoughts. There were many days that

Ester and I spent alone with journalist/writer Douglas Tavolaro, co-author of this book, to recapture this part of our life. It was just one more moment of innumerable memories shared with Douglas over the last ten years that enabled us to compose *Nothing to Lose 2*.

As in our first volume, this book is not simply a chronological retelling of events. It's a collection of stories of friends, co-workers in the church, those close to us, and those whose names we don't even know. The book does not follow a particular order. Most chapters were written out of sequence according to theme, for easier reading.

In *Nothing to Lose 2*, we explain how we were unjustly attacked, how we dealt with pressure, slander and prejudice, and how we overcame demeaning threats. We explain in detail a trial that few know about, a craving that turned into perseverance, persistence that turned into triumph, and all thanks to the faithfulness of the Word of God.

I would like to thank each one who participated in the book releases and bought our first book of memoirs.

May the stories in *Nothing to Lose 2* speak directly to your spirit. Happy reading!

CHAPTER 1

I WAS THE MIRACLE

God does not save from the furnace;
He saves from the fire.

DARK SKY

T he phone rang in the middle of the night, and I woke up with a start. Any call, I quickly imagined, meant a new attack, a new accusation of the press, more legal charges.

"Peace" was an unthinkable word at that time.

"Bishop, they don't want to talk. The owners will not accept our proposal. We have only a few days to find a way out," cautioned one of our lawyers in that call that was only seconds long.

After a day of exhausting meetings, the dining-room table at home was covered with documents spelling out how deep in debt we were from the purchase of TV Record. This call marked the end of one more round of negotiations that continued late into the night. The situation seemed like a puzzle with no solution. "My God, how do I put these pieces together? What should I do? How do we escape this maze?" My mind fought to find a way out.

It was the beginning of the 90's, in the first weeks of February. I knew that I had taken an audacious step—our first and truly great challenge. Either the Universal Church of the Kingdom of God would make a leap forward to radically change its story, or we would be knocked out by a blow that would destroy us. It was all or nothing! And I was at the forefront of it all.

The numbers were shocking. We bought Record for $45 million. Up to that point, it had been the largest business transaction we had ever made for a media outlet. It was uncommon for a radio and television station to be sold for that much money in our country. It was the price to pay for an unprecedented achievement.

It began with a down payment of $6 million. Another $8 million, the second part of the down payment, had to be paid within forty-five days. The remaining $31 million had to be paid to the previous owners over a period of two years—all in US dollars, and prorated to the current rates.

The Brazilian economy lived under the shadow of the monster of inflation, which predicted an uncertain future. Until today, I don't know how we did it. It didn't happen through conventional business procedures. In other words, there were no detailed calculations or financial research. I simply acted by faith. I believed and went ahead.

Right after the first payment, finances were tight. On the day the second payment was due, we still didn't have enough money, and worse, a clause in the contract stated that a late payment would cause me to forfeit the purchase of Record, and we'd lose any amount that had been paid up to that point. Not only did we not have the means for this down payment, other payments were coming due, which strangled us even more.

I needed a miracle.

I got home depressed that night. I shut the door to my room and sat on the bed in silence. I looked up at the ceiling. Through the window I could see the dark sky and took a deep breath. My Bible was on my bedside table, by the lamp. A sense of revolt burned inside of me. I spent practically the whole night just thinking. I thought of the power of God, and the possibility of turning the tables, of turning around impossible situations. I thought of the greatness of the Holy Spirit.

An intelligent faith that always guided my life and my surrender on the altar rose to the surface. How can I believe in a God so great, and live a life so miserable? This thought guided me and drove me to challenges thought impossible for any human being. When it comes to this, I've been radical. This has nothing to do with personal merit, being deserving, or having any great ability, but only believing in the promises of God and doing His will. That's what faith is.

It was this faith that I preached, and still preach, day and night. This is what I lived and still live with intensity. The prophet Joshua heard one of the most significant messages in the Bible, which speaks directly to me and empowers me in the most difficult moments. "No man shall be able to stand before you all the days of your life; as I was with Moses, so I will be with you. I will not leave you nor forsake you" (Joshua 1:6).

This promise, which has been displayed throughout the rooms of my home until today, brings certainty that I will find light at the end of the tunnel. We were facing a crisis. I never told this to anyone.

The next morning I woke up early and went to my office on the 13th floor of the Radio Copacabana building. On Visconde de Inhauma Ave., downtown Rio de Janeiro. I was restless. I was constantly pacing back and forth with apprehension. I asked myself, "What's the point of getting to this place and suddenly losing everything from one moment to the next?" I could not believe that God would abandon us halfway there, in the middle of this journey of high-risk challenges. "Why? Why God?" I agonized over these thoughts. There was a burden inside of me, something tormenting me—a deep dark anguish.

All of a sudden, as fast as a flash, I locked myself in the bathroom alone. It was the moment of decision.

I got on my knees, placed my face on the floor and cried. I unloaded all the weight I had on my shoulders. I had done everything I could do, and nothing had worked. Then I told God:

"Look God, the purchase of this station is in Your hands! If we buy Record, great. If we don't, we don't. Lord, you have to help me because I will not do anything more. I surrender."

I poured my heart out to God. It was only Him and me at that moment. My indignation burned with a supernatural force.

"My God, I have nothing to lose! Lord, You are my witness! This station is not for me."

My prayer was that short. My "amen" put a period at the end of my devastating affliction. When I got up, the crushing pressure in my chest had vanished. The skies seemed to have opened. I was glowing from within. I didn't know exactly what was going to happen, but the Holy Spirit had created inside of me an absolute certainty of His answer.

But I had to wait. There was no immediate solution in sight.

My words to God, unloaded in the bathroom of that building, represented the purest expression of what I had always imagined. I never wanted anything for myself, never had a personal agenda to pursue. But back in 1977, when the Universal Church began, I was certain that the growth of the gospel would need to depend on a means of mass communication to reach Brazil and the world.

The Lord Jesus preached in concert with the wind, almost always on mountaintops or hillsides, so that His voice would carry as far as possible. The majority of His miracles were done in public places, in full sight of many witnesses, so that these supernatural signs could spread throughout the population of Israel. These had been communication strategies used to reach a maximum amount of people.

. This was my thinking. TV, radio stations and mass media in general played an important role in the spread of the message of faith that I had known since I was young, in my first steps as a Christian. It was a dream of mine to win souls.

Since the first days of the Church, the sincerity of my intentions made me believe that God would place something extraordinary in our hands. When we didn't even have five minutes of purchase time on the radio, I would reiterate that some day we'd have a powerful TV station. On a certain night, when we were still in the first days of working in the old funeral parlor, in a meeting of at most 20 church members, I came up to the altar with a determination. I said a quick "good evening" and got straight to the point.

"People, listen carefully. Do you know that we're going to have our own television network?" I asked over the microphone.

The few people seated on the wooden pews looked at each other. One of the assistants standing against the wall smirked. In those days we had to sweat bullets just to pay our monthly rent.

"I mean it! We're going to be the owners of a large television station, and we'll be able to preach the gospel to the entire world. We're not going to have to depend on anyone, believe me! You can be sure of it."

This was not a moment of insanity. I spoke from a very clear conviction—an absolute conviction of the greatness of God that I believed in, and in His faithfulness to His Word. For me, this verse in the Bible was not just a vague promise, "The LORD of hosts has sworn, saying, 'Surely, as I have thought, so it shall come to pass, and as I have purposed, so it shall stand'" (Isaiah 14:24).

THE DAWN OF AN ERA

A short time after the beginning of the Universal Church back in 1978, one of our first members came and told me that she had been able to get us a fifteen-minute program on the radio. It was Mrs. Maria Veronese da Silva, who has now gone on to be with God, the wife of Mr. Albino, the same man who helped us find our first church building.

She agreed on a deal to pay the first three months of this radio program, 9,000 cruzeiros, the currency at that time, the exact same amount as our rent in the funeral parlor. In other words, after only a few months of starting the Church, we took on the challenge of doubling our monthly expenses, and so Radio Metropolitana in Rio de Janeiro became our first investment in communication.

"Evangelist Edir, the owner of the radio station accepted our offer. There's only one hitch. He'll only give us the last fifteen minutes of the night, after Baba Ivete Brum. Do you want it?" Maria asked timidly.

I was thrilled with the proposal. My yes was immediate. Ivete Brum was a well-known "babalorixá", a priestess in the type of witchcraft called candomblé, (common in Brazil and other Latin American countries) and had a program promoting this type of spiritism. This was a golden opportunity. Piggy-backing on the audience of this program before us, many listeners who had been deceived by witchcraft would certainly come to find out about the Universal Church's work of deliverance.

And that's just what happened. I began to speak about the truth of these spirits and to broadcast impressive life stories of people who had been transformed by God, and to challenge the results of the promises made by this witchdoctor. She attracted a huge amount of people by giving out a "happiness coin", and when I found out about this, I quickly reached out to her frustrated listeners who were seeing no results. The church meetings were packed out. The meetings in the funeral parlor began to overflow, and we became known as the church of miracles, a fact we'll go into more detail about in the chapter called, *A Giant Circle*.

Our program initially began at 10:45pm, but was extended to 45 minutes and played at 7 in the morning. In the future, we would rent out the whole of Radio Metropolitana 24 hours a day. But in October of 1978, six months after our pioneering investment in radio, we decided to stretch ourselves to reach more people and took a shot at renting out TV time.

This opportunity came by way of the now defunct TV Tupi, which even then was showing signs of a financial strain that led to its eventual bankruptcy. But at that time the station had a network of affiliates that fulfilled our plan for growth. The daily 30-minute program reached all of Brazil and was called "The Awakening of Faith."

Financially, it was too soon to branch out into television. But my belief and vision, thanks to the direction of God's Spirit, drove me to take the risk. Millions of Brazilians had televisions by the end of the 1970s, and the turn of that decade was marked by the advent of television.

"The Awakening of Faith" began at 7:30am, an hour that no other station had programming. In those days most channels were off the air until late morning. In other words, we were the only option for people who turned on their TVs at that time of day, which turned our program into a giant springboard for the meetings of the Universal Church.

The hand of God was there.

I recorded the programs myself in the main studios of TV Tupi, Channel 6, in the Urca neighborhood of Rio de Janeiro. Every Monday morning, without fail, we made five recordings at once. Our background set was a design of praying hands beneath rays of light.

I hosted a 15-minute interview segment called "Panel of Truth", which was followed by a prayer for workers and those who going through any kind of suffering, and continued with the same strategy we used on the radio. We threw our all into spreading the news about our bold faith and spiritual freedom. We were very careful in the testimonies we chose. Since I was involved in the church on a daily basis, our simple language and direct approach caught people's attention. But above all, our sincere desire to help those who felt lost won over a multitude of viewers.

Today TV evangelism is no longer the same. So many protestant pastors are speaking about their innumerable churches on their various programs during the day. Many are driven by a business mentality and sheer vanity, nothing more than false advertising. Their main objective is to attract members of other churches that began from nothing, that rely only on the anointing of God. In reality, few are worried about reaching the suffering. It's an avalanche of mindless programs, based on cheap emotional appeals, with the ultimate goal of "rescuing the suffering".

To take full advantage of our TV time, I recorded a vinyl album of Christian music in 1979 with a colored illustration of our "Awakening of Faith" logo on the cover. On one side we recorded the music, "Let's Pray Now", and on the other side, "A Prayer of Crying Out". That prayer communicated what I still ask for daily, up until today. Some of the phrases were:

"God, you know how many people are suffering, how many are in agony and are groaning. These people have been searching back and forth for answers, their feet aching and wounded.

Some are unable to call out or to ask You for help. They have cried out so many times already, and all that can be heard now is just a groan, a whisper.

My God, don't fail to listen to us at this moment. Your

Word guarantees that whatever we ask for in the name of the Lord Jesus Christ, we will receive.

Your Word confirms that the Lord takes pleasure in answering us. Lord, You take pleasure in answering us, and we have the faith to ask."

For years, the background music to this prayer had played on our radio program, but it was TV Tupi that made it so well known. Millions of Brazilian families came to the Universal Church because of this simple album.

When Tupi went bankrupt in July of 1980, we began regional programming in various stations, and in the main cities of Brazil, we used the Bandeirantes Network. By 1981, our program was being played in 20 different states. Neither today nor then would we abandon television in the preaching of the gospel or in caring for the needy. The "Awakening of Faith" marked the start of an era, and became a central pillar in the growth of the Universal Church.

⚬⚬⚬

In the Radio Copacabana building, I was in a time crunch, with the pressure of making the payments for TV Record. My prayers, short, full of revolt, in the bathroom of my office, strengthened me in this battle for the purchase of one of the biggest TV stations in the country. After my words of indignation to God, my spirit would be strengthened, yet I still couldn't figure out a way to pay the astronomical debt.

Brazil had just gone to the polls to elect its first president after a long military dictatorship, and waited anxiously for the possible political and economic changes that would come with the new government. Inflation was rampant and our bills would multiply from morning to afternoon on the same day. I was fearful of even looking at the exchange rate. We had no more credit in the banks, and had no one to run to.

I trusted only in the power of faith.

This strength drove me to believe in a miracle to prevent us from losing TV Record. The situation grew more unbearable by the moment, but I refused to give up.

BUT DON'T FORGET

W e grew in the 1980s because of the amount of time we bought on radio and TV, even though we hadn't reached the goal to own our own station. Then an opportunity came along to make a purchase: Radio Copacabana, one of the most popular and well-known AM stations of Rio de Janeiro at that time.

To pay for that purchase, I sold a house I had recently built in Petropolis. Our move to those mountains of Rio, where the town of Petropolis was nestled, had ushered in a special phase in the life of our family. That had been such a pleasant time, we had enjoyed many special moments together there.

I'd leave the church meetings in the neighborhood of Abolição in the 90 degree heat of the midday sun, but when I'd get to the foot of the mountains, the temperature would drop by 20 degrees. The mist would seep into the rooms of the house. After so many years living in north Rio, in tiny cramped apartments, I could finally give my wife Ester and my daughters a little comfort. But that didn't last long. The sale of our house was crucial to the purchase of Radio Copacabana.

I have bitter memories as well of our time in Petropolis, when we had to battle the asthma attacks of our oldest daughter, Cristiane, which have now been completely overcome over the years. Many nights I slept on the floor so that she could sleep in the arms of her mother.

Ester, on the other hand, would patiently drive the hourlong trip from the north of Rio to our house after the last meeting of the day, almost always in the middle of the night, without ever uttering one complaint. I would leave exhausted after an entire day of meetings, yet she always emanated patience and serenity.

Petropolis also brings back some very painful memories of an almost fatal car accident. It was a horrific scene. It was just after six in the morning, when I usually left the house for Radio Metropolitana. The street where I lived was one of the steepest slopes of the neighborhood. My driver had just filled the gas tank of our new car.

I was hit hard in the passenger seat where I sat. My driver was not yet used to this new vehicle, and the car flipped several times as it careened down the hill. I was thrown out of the car—until today, I don't know how—and was knocked unconscious as I landed.

The driver ran back to the house and told Ester that I was dead. Minutes later, I woke up stunned. I could not stand by myself. As I gained consciousness, I realized that the gas tank was leaking fuel. I was quickly rescued and taken to the emergency room at the hospital where I stayed for a few days. I had several serious fractures. I had a concussion with swelling, one arm was broken and the other one was badly dislocated. I had injuries all over my body.

The angels of God protected me. The Lord Jesus saved me from death.

Soon afterwards, we moved to a place in Barra da Tijuca to be closer to the church offices and to the studios of Radio Copacabana. The station required my frequent presence in its first years of operation, and I viewed this purchase as a milestone in the preaching of the gospel.

In July of 1984, we made an announcement to our church all over the country in an article in our church newspaper, entitled, "Radio Cobacabana is ours!" The title was a play on the 1958 World Cup victory of the Brazilian soccer team. Below, I have an excerpt from the declaration signed by me and celebrated by all of us, as if we had won the World Cup trophy.

"There were many prayers, requests and fasts. We lived in faith and expectation of this moment.

We didn't give up! We didn't lose hope! Not even for a moment did we weaken.

And we remained firm walking step by step together with Him, confident that we would achieve our dream: the purchase of a radio station where we could practice our faith in the Lord's Work.

We want to instill the name of Jesus into the hearts of listeners far and wide. Our gracious God has heard and answered our prayers and has given the Universal Church the privilege of seeing everyone's dream come true.

For this purpose, we are bending over backwards and taking on more work. All the church members, pastors, and our radio station team are united and pulling together.

Radio Copacabana is ours!
Bishop Macedo"

These words have become a reality. For the first years, I personally made the late night programs. I spent hour after hour talking to listeners with the most varied types of suffering. From Monday through Friday, my broadcasts began at midnight and ended at four in the morning. During the day, I led meetings in the church, and many times helped in other radio programs in the mornings or afternoons, and Ester was always by my side.

I was always exhausted. But that spiritual help in the early morning hours saved many people from hell. Stories abound of faithful members and even pastors of the Universal Church today, who were rescued over the airwaves of Radio Copacabana.

This power has multiplied in Brazil over the years. We either bought airtime or purchased new radio stations all over the country, north and south. The reach of this vehicle of communication gave rise to our initial growth. We were accessible to the general population, from the most remote communities to the largest cities. At that time, radio was vital for the spread of the Word of God within the country.

Today there are hundreds of hours of daily broadcasts through the different stations that make up our Alleluia Network. I always make a point of broadcasting my program live throughout Brazil every day at 11pm. When I'm visiting our churches in other countries, I always find a time during the day to record my message. This is sacred. I always carry a device with me wherever I go that allows me to send a recording over the Internet from anywhere in the world.

It's been a pleasure to dedicate myself to this radio program from the beginning until now. I wonder how many millions of people have been saved, pulled back from the edge of a deep pit with a fresh breath of air to transform their lives, after hearing a word from those broadcasts. A simple word. Many were rescued from despair at such times, all alone and in utter darkness.

It moves me to think about this. God has given us the privilege of helping thousands of people who are depressed, who have suicidal thoughts, who are sick, who are addicts, and who are tormented by so much evil while others peacefully sleep. Reaching out to those in need draws us near to God: "For thus says the High and Lofty One who inhabits eternity, whose name is Holy: 'I dwell in the high and holy place, with him who has a contrite and humble spirit, to revive the spirit of the humble, and to revive the heart of the contrite ones'" (Isaiah 57:15).

This passage speaks to me so deeply that I include it in my email signature. But before that passage, I add the words, "But don't forget." Much more than a self-help message, these words motivate me and give me a reason to exist.

THE ULTIMATE PROPHECY

The saga of the purchase of Record that had brought pain and worry beyond anything I could ever have imagined, with bills far beyond our financial means, began with a phone call after I had moved to the United States to preach the gospel.

"Bishop, Record Network is for sale. One of our lawyers gave me this information firsthand," said Paulo Roberto Guimarães, one of the oldest bishops, who was responsible for the Universal Church in Brazil at that time.

"The opportunity looks great, Paulo. Let's proceed immediately," I answered with conviction. "We need to be careful and do everything properly so that this chance doesn't pass us by."

After hanging up the phone, the significance of that special moment would not leave my mind. What would the purchase of a TV channel with the brand and tradition of TV Record mean? As always, I remembered my encounter with God. This was not a project for being pretentious.

The Holy Spirit probed my mind and knew my intentions. There was a genuine faith and revolt inside of me.

What gave rise to my indignation was seeing so many Brazilians far from God, thirsting for eternal salvation. I could already imagine what a TV station would mean for the plans of God. How many could be rescued? How many lives could be restored? How many miracles could happen? The Work of God would never be the same.

I also remembered something that had happened more than one year before, on 27th March 1988. It had been the last time I had determined in public that we would be the owners of a big television station. It had been in a packed Maracanã stadium at the grand opening of TV Rio, channel 13, bought at that time by Pastor Nilson do Amaral Fanini, former president of the Worldwide Baptist Alliance.

To mark the start of the new programming at the station, a special meeting had been organized and attended by pastors from several different denominations and by politicians. There was just one problem. The stadium would be empty.

"Bishop Edir, I need a big favor. Can you help me fill Maracanã?" asked Fanini by phone. "You know how it is. Only the Universal Church has the ability to fill up the seats of Maracanã."

I took the call with some suspicion, but took his words at face value.

"We'll broadcast the meeting live. It'll be a beautiful ceremony, Bishop Edir. We need to show the strength of the Protestant Church," said the Baptist pastor.

"Okay, I only need your help to print up the announcements for our people." I responded with a follow-up question:

"What will this meeting be like, Pr. Fanini?"

"First we'll present a show and announce the new schedule, then call the Minister of Communication to announce the official opening of the new TV Rio. Right after that, I'll hand the microphone to you to make whatever comments you want and then end the live transmission."

On the day, over 40,000 filled the seats and chairs on the field where the large stage for the ceremony had been erected. The overwhelming majority of people were of course, members and staff of the Universal Church throughout the state of Rio. The event began with a prayer from other pastors and a gospel music concert.

I was sitting onstage next to Ester over on one corner. Seated in front of me were Christian speakers from different denominations and places, some even from the United States. All of a sudden, they presented a dance troupe of candomblé and umbanda, types of traditional witchcraft. Men and women all in white danced and twirled to the sound of drums. I couldn't believe my eyes, and the people of the Universal Church were shocked. The sound of people booing began to swell around the Maracanã stadium. I could not stop laughing.

Fanini continued the ceremony and presented the board of directors of his station, and gave lavish praise to Walter Clark, a famous television executive responsible for the programming of TV Rio. He resigned days later over a misunderstanding with Fanini. Then Fanini announced the presence of the Minister of Communication, Antonio Carlos Magalhães, who landed on the field in a helicopter and walked on foot to the stage. When he got to the center of the field, the national anthem was played by the navy band.

I thought to myself, "Now it's my turn. Let's pray and give the people some faith. Let's shake this stadium up." I was counting the seconds for that bureaucratic presentation to end. The minister ended his speech and to my surprise, contrary to our agreement, Fanini called up another musical group. The people in the stands started calling our names, but nothing changed. More prayers were made by other pastors. Added to the spectacle was a flock of doves and shower of rose petals. I was still sitting in the background next to Ester as I had been since the beginning of the event.

After two hours of waiting, I was finally called forward. Fanini thanked me for being there, the other Christian leaders, the politicians, and believe it or not, announced the end of the broadcast. Only after the program went off the air, was I called to speak. I was enraged. I took the microphone and, as all the other speakers were leaving the stage and entered the tunnel to leave the field, I started a chorus of a song with all the people in the stadium:

"My faith has great power by the grace of Jesus Christ! Every demon must get out, because they can't resist the light. Out! Out! Out!"

The stands were stirred up. I began to preach about the quality of a true belief that forces God to manifest. And in a burst of faith, still affected by the indignation of being treated unfairly, I proclaimed that this TV channel would be ours. I stated categorically that God would place it in our hands.

In spite of the embarrassment I suffered, a month later I forgave Pastor Fanini. Four years after that day in Maracanã in February 1993, TV Rio was purchased by members of the Universal Church, and today has been transformed into TV Record Rio de Janeiro, one of the main stations that make up the Record Network.

THE UNEXPECTED

In the days following the call of Paulo Roberto Guimarães to my house in New York, I realized that this was a chance to see a prophecy fulfilled that had been spoken by me throughout my ministry as a preacher of the Word of God. So as not to lose this opportunity to purchase Record, we needed to act with swiftness and intelligence.

In a serious financial crises, the station was on the verge of bankruptcy. The owners at the time, the entrepreneur and TV personality, Silvio Santos, and the Machado de Carvalho family, ran Record under a large debt. The deficit was huge. The company grossed 200 million a year, and had 20 million dollars in outstanding bills. In the closing balance of 1989, Record would not be able to stay afloat. The one who revealed these facts to us was Demerval Gonçalves, a trustworthy man of the Silvio Santos group at that time and responsible for the sale, and now an executive at TV Record.

I was constantly kept up to date about the newest changes in the various interested parties in the TV market. Various media groups in Brazil and abroad were interested in Record. The list was long, but I was confident in the desire that had been created in me, just as Paul the Apostle affirmed, "For it is God who works in you both to will and to do for His good pleasure" (Philippians 2:13).

I quickly returned from New York to Brazil and called a meeting with the pastor and former congressman, Laprovita Vieira, the same man that would accompany me on the day of my arrest, three years later.

"I would like you to go to São Paulo and buy Record. Go ahead and seal the deal, Vieira," I said drily. "Can I count on you?" He was taken aback.

"Buy Record? THE Record, right? Okay Bishop, you can count on me," he responded with a voice of someone who had just heard the absurd.

At the meeting with Demerval Gonçalves at the old station on Miruna Ave., in São Paulo, Vieira announced that he was interested in buying Record. I had asked him to be emphatic.

"I want to buy the station, right now," said Vieira to Demerval.

The negotiations progressed rapidly, the proposal pleased the partners of Record, and they called a meeting at the house of Silvio Santos. It was the first of an unending round of discussions. I knew that if I appeared, the negotiations would be overpriced and possibly undone by prejudice. Everything could be lost.

Because of this, Vieira attended all meetings with a pack of cigarettes on display in his shirt pocket. No one suspected that I was behind this all-important purchase. I was deter-mined not to appear—only in an extreme case.

This extreme case appeared after we had closed the deal and when we were unable to pay the second part of the de-posit. There was only one solution. Renegotiate the debt with Silvio Santos. Our meeting took place in his old offices, on Jaceguai St., in Bela Vista, São Paulo.

It was with Silvio Santos, his partner, and Vieira, along with the lawyers of both parties. In the middle of the meet-ing, they reached a deadlock. Everyone was talking about new terms and values without any agreement in sight. That's when I stood up from one of the chairs in the office and said:

"We can stop this discussion. I'm Bishop Macedo. I'm the one behind the purchase of Record. Let's resolve this once and for all. What can we do?" I asked.

The representative of Silvio Santos gave a price.

I responded by faith.

"Not a problem. The deal's done."

I was impatient with the progress of the transaction. I had gone disguised as Vieira's driver to wield my gavel in case the negotiations got out of hand. I thought that by identifying my-self, I could resolve the problem, always in a spirit of prayer and confident that God was taking care of the entire situation.

But even so, the agreement did not go through. That same week, Silvio Santos said that he had regrets, but that he was bound by the deposit that Vieira had made and under pressure to balance Record's debt.

That's when the lawyers called me at home in the mid-dle of the night with a negative response to our negotiations, recounted at the beginning of this book. The next day when I left the office at Radio Copacabana, where I had prayed on my knees seeking a decision from God, I tried to follow my normal routine in the church, but it was impossible. A calculator spelled fear to me.

I decided to speak to Silvio Santos personally to renegotiate the debt. But when he received the message, he resisted one more time. He refused from the start, and said that if that were the case, he would return the money already paid and take back Record. The conversation lasted for hours.

"If I have to return the money, I'll return it and keep the station," Silvio told me.

"I don't want the money back. I don't want your money. I want to pay what I owe. I want to renegotiate the rest of the payments," I responded.

Our finances kept getting leaner. Our financial situation was getting tighter by the day. The press had already published that the sale of Record had been suspended because of a failure to pay the purchase price that had been laid out in the letter of intent signed by Vieira. They printed that the board of directors would only send the document of transfer to the Ministry of Communication after the negotiations were finalized with the agreed payments.

A spiritual war broke out. When my part in the purchase of Record became known, the attacks intensified. A discriminatory tone dominated the flood of news reports. There was a clear attempt to block me with lawsuits and subpoena after subpoena. They began to investigate my life and my family, but no accusations were ever proven.

I never imagined that I would go through such hell from the day that I decided to buy Record. The attacks came from all sides. It seemed like a plot to block me from achieving anything great that would transform the history of the Church. It was a spiritual battle to block millions of people from being rescued from the darkness.

How could we pay off so much debt? Where would help come from? Who would protect us? Prayer and crying out became my daily expressions. Not even Ester knew for certain the size of the hole in my chest.

In some meetings it was hard for me to preach. I would go up on the altar and just pour out my tears to God. I hardly had the strength to cry out. Minutes would pass and I'd be paralyzed after looking at the enormity of the bills. I ran to the Bible in search of a solution. "The LORD is righteous in her midst, He will do no unrighteousness. Every morning He brings His justice to light; He never fails, but the unjust knows no shame" (Zephaniah 3:5).

He would not fail. I needed to find a way out. The situation was extreme. That prayer in Radio Copacabana. That crying out to God. The interminable wait. Would the prophecies finally be fulfilled?

On Friday 15th March 1990, one day after the inauguration of President Fernando Collor de Melo, a gigantic glimmer of light appeared. TV news reports were announcing live the implementation of the Collor Plan. It was the most ambitious and drastic economic package created to halt inflation. It was a plan so radical in its methods and so painful to the pocketbooks of those who had any savings in the bank.

Those who had more than 50,000 new cruzados (the modern equivalent of $2,000) in savings and checking accounts were to have their money confiscated. It was the most shocking part of the changes in the economy. They failed to produce any results for the future, unless you count the tragedies in people's lives. From one day to the next, millions of Brazilians ran out of money, even for medical treatment. The consequences for many families were irreparable: death, unemployment and suicide.

The economic package which terrorized most Brazilians was a relief for me. Of course I deplored the suffering and loss of each victim of the Collor Plan. I was angry at how it tortured people. But amidst all this turmoil, it meant something different to me.

Silvio Santos and his partners were unable to pay off Record's debts, which forced them to strike an urgent deal. Their creditors threatened to file bankruptcy. The money was stuck in litigation and would only be released when the contract was enforced.

Days after the closing of the deal came other surprising news. Lawyers informed me that the plan had caused a drop in the value of the loan payments due to a brutal devaluation of the dollar. The payments of Record's purchase, which were based on foreign exchange rates, plummeted. Debts that had previously been exorbitant collapsed.

It seemed unbelievable. I redid the math. I turned my thoughts to God and thanked Him.

We began to pay the installments with enormous ease, to the point that we would pay up to three in a single month. Before 1992, our debt was paid in full. Record was ours.

How do I explain this incredible turnaround? How did it happen? Everyone can believe what they want—I have the absolute certainty that it was an act of God.

But today, even more important than becoming the owners of the second largest media group in Brazil, and one of the largest in the world, was the spiritual experience gained by walking that thorny path of great hardship. The Holy Spirit guided us throughout the journey, in spite of the unimaginable weakness we felt at the moment. Had I put my hope in human beings, I would not have been saved. The miracle had to begin with me.

Faith brought the unreal into existence.

The impossible happened.

CHAPTER 2

A JOURNEY OF DISCOVERIES

"Now to Him who is able to do exceedingly abundantly above all that we ask or think, according to the power that works in us."

(Ephesians 3:20)

THE GIANT CIRCLE

Everyone's eyes followed the movement of my hands. I entered in silence and went straight to the blackboard. It was the advanced class of the recently opened Universal Church School of Theology that operated in an old building in north Rio, where everything had begun.

After a greeting, I drew a small dot with some white chalk. The students were curious, and looked at each other, wondering what was coming next. Then I drew a big circle around the small dot.

"Do you know what this is?" I asked in a further attempt to arouse their interest.

No one hazarded a guess, so I continued.

"This is the Universal Church. Today we're a dot, but tomorrow, we'll become a big circle. Believe my words, this is going to happen!"

Then I began a lesson about the importance of believing in the impossible, based on teachings and doctrines as the Word of God explains. Like the story behind the purchase of our TV and radio stations, the unusual growth of the Universal Church of the Kingdom of God throughout Brazil and the world was determined when we only had 20 people at the small pavilion and at the meetings in the old funeral parlor.

Biblical faith demands that we reason. "Now faith is the substance of the things hoped for, the evidence of things not seen" (Hebrews 11:1). I knew what I wanted and what could happen with a boundless confidence in the God of Abraham, Moses and Joshua. This was not mere bravado. I always insisted on the promises of the Bible being fulfilled.

"Our church will be big because God is big. I refuse to believe in a big and powerful God, and then see His Church as withered, tied up and small. This work is going far," I preached in meetings with an attendance that I could count on my fingers.

From the altar, I could see nine or ten faithful members, and determined to preach for millions of people around the world. I was unwavering in my convictions with the first pastors as well. One Monday morning I called a meeting with our main pastors on the second floor of our church in Abolição, and after a talk about the gospel, I was very frank. At that time we were a small group.

"You know, it's so good to be together like this. We're family. Because of this, we find so much joy in these get-togethers, this unity," I stated with joy.

Then I concluded:

"It's a shame that in a short time from now, it won't be like this. The Universal Church is going to grow so much that it will be hard to talk to each other or get together. This type of gathering will be rare."

Many of these pastors are now, in fact, spread out through various continents of the world, and all remember the words of that morning. Those idealistic bold statements were not based on any virtue or superior skills, but were based on the fact that reason could not allow me to believe that the one who created the heavens and the earth would not respond to me in the same magnitude of His creative power.

I'm not superhuman.

This mindset produced a spirit of revolt inside of me day and night that will be with me until my very last breath. It's in my blood.

I tried to communicate this to everyone around me in a clear, emphatic way. It was this faith that drove me to give up the security and benefits of a government job, against the advice of everyone and everything, to dedicate myself to the altar. It enabled me to overcome the defeatism of other denominations whose leaders did not believe in me. It gave me the strength to overcome the sickness of my beloved daughter, Viviane. It had enabled me to overcome the limitations of the pavilion to find the old funeral parlor. It had guided me to have a true encounter with God and the baptism in the Holy Spirit. It had given me a passion for souls, a new zest for life, and enabled me to reach where I had never gone before.

I had nothing to lose.

From the beginning, my dedication to the church was round-the-clock, tireless. I quickly moved to a small apartment next to the old funeral home to be available 24/7 for people's spiritual needs. I gave all I had, all of the time. I made meetings morning, afternoon and evening.

I counseled dozens of people every week, hundreds per month, before and after the meetings, and would visit the homes and businesses of the church members. Our visits also included hospitals, slums and low-income areas of town, making prayers and giving simple, direct messages of faith. I always understood that people are more important than anything else.

Even so, the Church did not grow immediately. I often walked into meetings staring down at the floor, or even with my eyes closed, to avoid feeling discouraged. Some meetings in the middle of the day would only have four or five people. I held onto a verse in the Bible to help me see what was not visible.

"Jesus said, 'For where two or three are gathered together in my name, I am there in the midst of them.'" So I'd immediately announce, "Jesus is here among us. Do you believe it?" I would ask, inviting the few that were present to hold hands for a quick prayer.

In this manner, standing in front of the pulpit, I led some of my best meetings. I listened to the problems and frustrations of each one of them and determined an answer from God.

And so, the Church grew. We started making meetings in cinemas and public squares, in other neighborhoods of Rio de Janeiro. I would stay up late into the night with other volunteers, printing flyers on a mimeograph machine, which

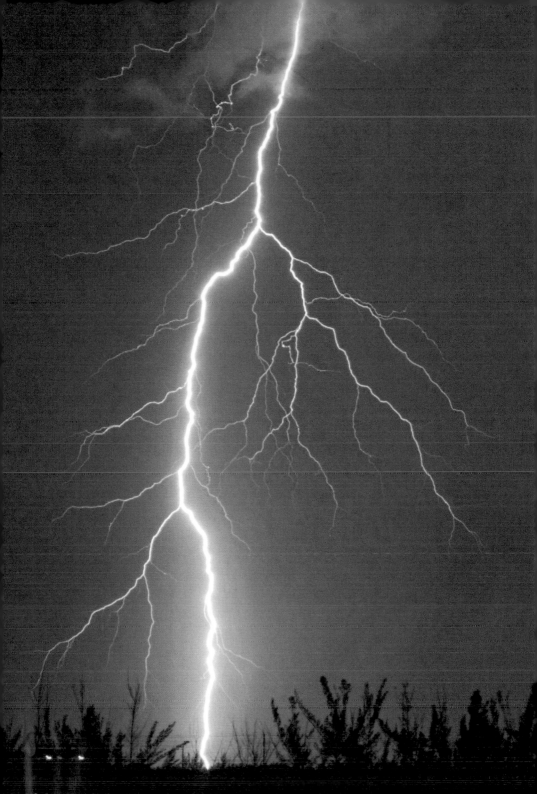

Faith is like a lightning bolt. It happens suddenly, in the blink of an eye, striking evil with a force that's out of the ordinary.

São Paulo, 6 de novembro de 1989.

À
Rádio Record S/A
At.: Dr. Paulo Machado de Carvalho Fº

Nesta

Prezado Senhor:

Sabedor do propósito de V.Sa. e dos demais acionistas dessa empresa em desfazerem-se das ações de que são possuidores, sirvo-me da presente para manifestar minha intenção em adquirí-las, condicionando-se tal desiderato, como de praxe, ao prévio e detalhado conhecimento da situação econômico-financeira daquela sociedade.

Na expectativa de um breve pronunciamento de V.Sa. para que possamos dar início aos entendimentos, subscrevo-me,

atenciosamente.

ODENIR LAPROVITA VIEIRA

The Letter of Intent for the purchase of Record Network in 1989. The oldest active broadcaster was transformed into the second largest television station of Brazil.

Cristina Rufatto

Silvio Santos, Laprovita e Edir Macedo aguardando para depor no Fórum

Negotiations with Silvio Santos marked the beginning of a series of attacks, undoubtedly one of the most difficult moments of my life.

TV TUPI

In 1978 the program, "The Awakening of Faith" pioneered on former TV-Tupi. On the "Panel of Truth" I presented never-before-seen testimonies. – An LP that characterized those times in the lives of many members.

When I first started preaching, I relied on the precious help of the women of Home Missionaries, who distributed flyers and helped grow the Church.

Igreja Universal do Reino de Deus
SEDE: Av. Suburbana, 7.258 – Tel 269-6945
Rio de Janeiro – CGC 29.744.778/0001-97
(MISSIONÁRIA) MEMBRO

NOME *Bebiana Moreira Affonso*

Igreja *Jacarepaguá* .... Inscrição N.º ....002..

Igreja Universal do Reino de Deus

Assinatura do Pastor
Diretor-Presidente

MILHARES DE PESSOAS ESTÃO SENDO ATENDIDAS POR DEUS,
ATRAVÉS DAS ORAÇÕES QUE SÃO FEITAS EM NOME DE JESUS,

"Tudo é possível para aquele que crê". (Jesus Cristo)

O pastor MACEDO e sua equipe de fé, convida todos os necessitados para receberem a Prece Poderosa.

Venha unir sua fé à do "Pastor" MACEDO e sua equipe, para receber "As Graças de Deus".

PASTOR MACEDO

Diariamente às 9:00, às 15:00 e às 20:00 horas

Av. Suburbana, 7258 – Abolição – A 20 metros do Largo da Abolição

Pastor Rodrigues

Evangelista Rena

——————— PRECE INVENCÍVEL ———————

Ó Grande, Invencível e Poderoso Deus dos Exércitos, em o Nome do Senhor Jesus eu me levanto contra todo o mal que me assedia. Eu uso ó Deus, o Nome dos nomes, o Nome de Seu amado filho, para repreender todas as forças estranhas e ocultas que estão tentando me derrubar. E através da minha fé naquele que é o mesmo, ontem, hoje e o será para sempre, isto é, o Senhor Jesus Cristo, eu já me considero liberto a partir deste momento em diante, porque Nosso Senhor Jesus me garante o milagre, pois Ele disse que tudo quanto pedíssemos a Ti em Seu nome, Tu atenderias! Portanto,

todo e qualquer mal que me assola, saia agora! Agora mesmo! Em nome de Jesus! Obrigado Senhor, pois já posso ver a luz; obrigado Senhor, porque já posso sorrir. Ó Graças a Deus, ó Graças a Ti Senhor Jesus! Ó Graças a Ti Senhor, que inclinas os teus ouvidos para atender a um desmerecido! Agora Senhor, eu posso afirmar que só o Senhor é Deus. Toma-me neste momento e faça de mim um vaso de bênçãos, em o Nome do Senhor Jesus!

Amém Senhor... Amém

Faça a Prece Invencível com os missionários, através da Rádio Metropolitana, diariamente às 7:00 h (da manhã) e às 22:55 h (de 2ª a 6ª feira).

Bishop Paulo Roberto Guimarães was responsible for the evangelistic work in Bahia, that began on Tijolo Road, in those days, a filthy, violent area of town.

Days after his marriage in 1979, the late Bishop Renato Maduro was sent to Juiz de Fora, Minas Gerais, to open on of our first churches outside of Rio de Janeiro.

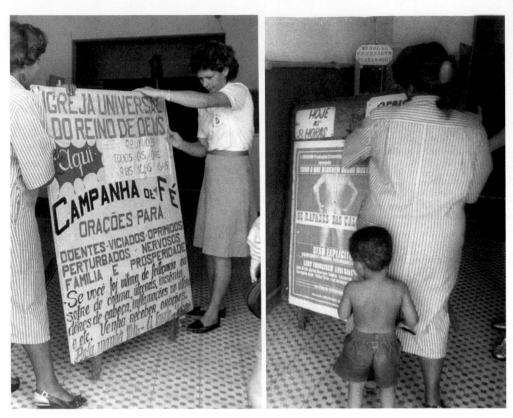

As the church grew, we started to use cinema halls that showed pornographic films. Below, an ID card for the UCKG's theological courses, FATURD.

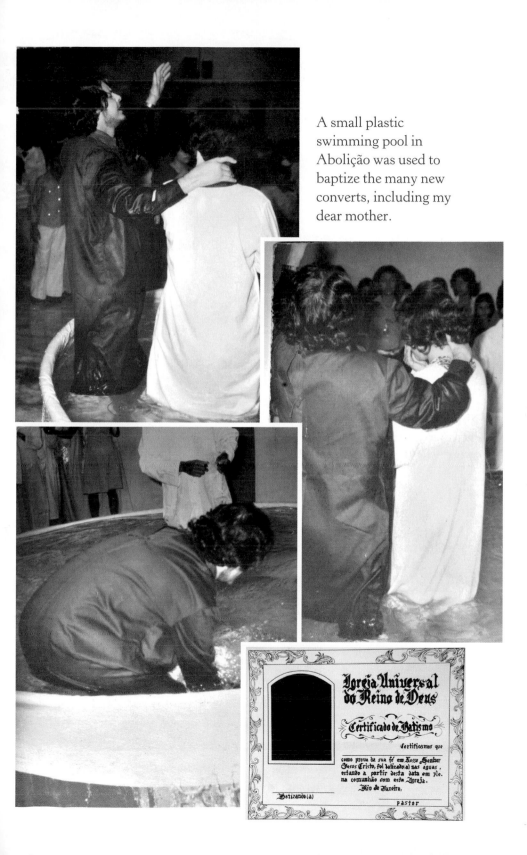

A small plastic swimming pool in Abolição was used to baptize the many new converts, including my dear mother.

A IGREJA DO

Aspecto do interior do Templo, durante uma Reunião

After a short period of work, the simple warehouse of the old furniture factory on Avenida Suburbana, in Rio de Janeiro, became known as "the Church of Miracles."

MILAGRES

The meetings in Abolição were packed with so many people that
the heat caused the walls to drip with moisture.

Antiga Igreja em Abolição - RJ

From the
earliest days, my
dedication to
the church was a
tireless, 24-hour
a day passion,
which continues
until today.

I sacrificed the house I had built in Petrópolis in order to see a dream come true: the purchase of Radio Copacabana.

The event in Maracanã for the opening of the former TV Rio. In an act of faith I stated that the station would be ours.

My girls and I dance during a meeting in the Church. Ester was always the solid base of our family.

I gave up the pleasure of being close to my small children for the sake of a faith that embraced all. Our family is on the altar.

we gave out during the day on the streets and in business areas. We developed our own method for the training of pastors and evangelists (assistant pastors). There were few of us, which made it easier to personally keep track of how they were doing.

It was brick by brick. On the altar, I would interview those who had seen miracles or whose lives had been transformed. Those who heard were amazed; the stories spread. Those who attended invited others, who then invited others, and others and others. The numbers multiplied. Everyone wanted to discover the secret of a faith that could do anything.

"Before all, we need to believe in ourselves. If you believe in God but don't believe in yourself, your belief in God won't work. Think along with me. If you believed in God, in a pure and simple way, the world would be a wonderful place. There's no other path for your success. You need to believe in God, and in yourself. The Spirit of God does not work alone. He needs partners in this world in order to do His wonders. He needs you to believe in Him and in yourself. This partnership makes the impossible possible. You need to believe in who you are. This is the first step to live by faith in the God of Abraham, of Isaac and of Israel," I would say in meetings.

In this manner, living what I preached, I was able to resist those doubts that flew in the face of our initial efforts. Some relatives, in particular, my brother-in-law Romildo Ribeiro Soares, always said that it would never work. But I paid no attention to his words, I just kept going forward.

Soares began the Church with me because he wanted the work to grow quickly by importing pastors from other denominations. Many were unemployed, had no commitment and had bad marriages. It would never work.

I knew that the secret was to make disciples that the Church itself would give birth to, rescued by the same faith that they had embraced from the very beginning. It would be necessary to help them to grow. Under no conditions would I accept pastors who were not yet spiritually free. Only time would ensure quality. Clearly, this difference of thought caused a separation in our work, and caused the two of us to part ways in the Work of God, as described in *Nothing to Lose 1*.

The old funeral parlor had space for 225 people in the pews. But some meetings would be packed with more than 400. The lines of people who wanted counseling were enormous and criss-crossed the aisles. At times, I spent hours giving counsel to just one person. I took on the battles of each one, with prayer and guidance by the light of God's Word. Many people would knock on my window in the middle of the night to ask for help. I would come home from the meetings exhausted, ready for sleep, and they asked me for help. That's what happened with the sister of a young girl who lived on a neighboring street.

"Pastor, wake up, for the love of God! My sister is manifesting a terrible demon at home. She's out of control, help me!" begged the girl.

When I entered the house, it looked like a horror movie. She appeared to be a middle-aged woman who looked completely disfigured. Her body was distorted, her hands were twisted, and her eyes had rolled up under her lids. Her voice was rough, her demonic laughter could be heard from far away. On the floor was a torn Bible. People from other churches had tried to help her by placing a Bible on her head, but the unclean spirit just shredded it to bits like confetti. She regained consciousness shortly after we confronted the evil inside of her.

After listening to people for several years, I learned about the anguish of those who suffer. Every counseling session was a new lesson. I would learn something different every day in my talks with those in despair, which is what inspired me to decide that each day of the week, we would care for a specific type of need in our meetings. This seemed to be the best way to channel the faith of people who were searching for a certain type of help. We prioritized the meetings for salvation on Wednesday nights, and on Sunday mornings and afternoons.

This explosion of people came about after a massive effort to spread our work of deliverance during the first months of our radio program, which was still in Rio, as we will uncover in the pages to come. As we confronted spirits, we opened the eyes of those who were held hostage to the work of these evil forces. The old funeral parlor became small, with people spilling out onto the sidewalk. The main meetings were packed.

The fame of the Church spread.

Church members waited for the message on Fridays. I always illustrated the message with props or a skit to put people at ease and to reinforce what was being taught. One day, a young Pastor Manoel Francisco da Silva, now one of the oldest bishops of the Church, appeared on the altar in a skirt. He acted the part of a spirit known as "pomba-gira" (a demon that causes sexual immorality of a feminine nature). His hairy legs made the whole church shake with laughter.

We created an outreach called the "Home Missionaries", made up of women who spent their week offering help to those who were new in the faith. Many church members would be weakened through their day-to-day struggles, but were quickly helped by this group of volunteers. This was essential to create a firm group of new members. In many situations, a hug, a smile, or a simple, "Don't give up, God's with you," helped strengthen these beginners.

Everyone gave a little to help cover our expenses.

"The expenses of the Church were carefully kept track of so we wouldn't be late with our rent payment at the end of the month. Pastor Macedo was very insistent on being faithful in our payments. He didn't like to owe anything," remembers Solange Guimarães, one of our first administrative assistants, and wife of Bishop Paulo Roberto Guimarães, one of the Universal Church pioneers as well.

"When we had enough offering to pay the monthly rent in one meeting, it was an unforgettable joy. We bought sodas and pastries to celebrate," remembers Solange. "It seems small, but it was a big deal in those early days."

The fervor of the Church spread to everyone. In the early morning hours after prayer vigils, we would all get together to help clean the toilets and the auditorium of the church.

We only had half a dozen helping hands. Ester and I were always close. Even with our inexperience, we were very sincere in helping people—a work so small, but done with such great love. I believe the Holy Spirit saw those moments of profound dedication, care and respect for this work.

In all that we (and our volunteers) did, there were purity and self-sacrifice, which still exist today. Moments, unseen by anyone, hours bent over the duties of various tasks, often alone, in that old stuffy building of the funeral parlor.

I'm sure that the Universal Church is what it is today because of that zeal and affection.

A MORNING IN
THE CEMETERY

L ater, a tragedy affected me, and the church. A young pastor named Julio Cezar Gomes, 23 years of age, was traveling through a suburb of the city with the offerings of our people. He was a go-getter, a hard worker and very dedicated to the work of the gospel. He had been born into humble circumstances, tormented by depression and had been healed by the power of faith. Our church in Realengo had been opened for just a short time, but little by little, had grown and overcome the difficulties common at that time.

Halfway through his bus trip, an armed robbery took all the passengers by surprise. Julio Cezar was startled. His reluctance to lose the donations that he had packed into a bag on his shoulder caused him to panic. The thief shouted about the hold-up again. One by one, he collected wallets, purses, watches, rings and other valuables.

In an unexpected reaction, Pastor Julio refused to let go of the bag. The thief did not think twice, and fired. The pastor drew a few breaths and then collapsed. He was taken to the hospital where he died. He died practically embracing the offerings and tithes of the people.

The blood of the pastor was poured out to protect the blood of the church.

The crime shocked me. Our small church in Realengo went into mourning. That night, I reflected on the attitude of the pastor. Clearly, we never encourage anyone to resist during a robbery. The Bible teaches us to watch and pray (Ephesians 6:18), but the desire of that young man to protect the people's offering touched me.

The Holy Spirit has always guided the Universal Church in this way: understanding the holiness of the offering that is given in God's House. The money placed on the altar is as holy as the Bible itself—as holy as God. It represents the offering of God for the world, His Son, Jesus Christ.

The next day, I decided to go to the funeral of the young pastor, in the Ricardo de Albuquerque Cemetery in the northern zone of Rio. The body had been at an all-night wake. Upon entering, I saw grieving family members and inconsolable pastors and members of the Realengo church. The scene was very moving.

I greeted everyone. At the burial site, I read in a loud voice a psalm of David. "Precious in the sight of the LORD is the death of His saints" (Psalm 116:15). Then I had an unexpected reaction. I called the other pastors and asked them to help me lift the coffin up high and said a prayer.

I was direct with God:

"My Lord, today we have taken a blow. We've lost one of the soldiers of Your army. May his blood be multiplied into thousands of other lives, thousands of men of God around the world, to preach your Word."

Partly because of that moment, an army of preachers of the gospel has formed with the faith and mindset of the Universal Church, that has now multiplied throughout the world. Today we have over 11,000 pastors and wives in Brazil alone, and more than twice that amount worldwide. People of various races, cultures and languages under the direction of one Spirit, who you will come to learn about in the third volume of Nothing to Lose.

They are our greatest asset and have helped me from the very beginning in this long journey of the Church's growth and achievements.

In the former funeral parlor, growth forced me to make a decision: leave the old property for a larger building, a furniture factory on the same road, 7702 Suburbana Ave., also in the Rio de Janeiro neighborhood of Abolição. The grand opening of the new church took place in May 1980. I dealt directly with the owner, an Inhauma businessman.

After the change, with the growing popularity of our radio program, we reached a point where we would have more than 300 newcomers at times of the day that, until then, had little activity, which were Tuesday mornings and Friday afternoons. The deliverance meetings had people lined up on the sidewalk and caused the walls of the new building to drip with condensation. The heat and the number of people, more than 1,500, made us drip with sweat. The rent was expensive for us at that time, but we accepted the challenge. The old funeral parlor, which we used to house a printing press and our school for pastors, added to our expenses.

At first, the new Abolição church did not even have a baptistry, where water baptisms are performed for those who decide to accept the gospel. Like hundreds of other people, my mother, Geninha, was personally baptized by me in a small wading pool. Such a sweet memory. It was also in that church that I was consecrated to the position of bishop alongside Ester.

The ceremony took place in a meeting celebrating the third anniversary of the Universal Church, and was a joint decision of the board of pastors. The goal was to appoint an administrative head, but most of all, a spiritual leader. The decision was made by the 12 consecrated pastors at that time, who were later appointed bishops because of the growth of the Church. A bishop in the Universal Church is not a lifelong position, but rather one of trust, and should line up with the description in the first book of Timothy: "A bishop then must be blameless, the husband of one wife, temperate, sober-minded, of good behavior, hospitable, able to teach" (1 Timothy 3:2).

At the time of consecration, one of the pastors spoke about milestones in my ministry as a pastor and justified the need for a leader of the Church. My parents watched the whole thing. We knelt to receive the special anointing. Ester and I cried a great deal.

It was the fulfillment of my dream to serve God. How can we not remember the struggles to get there? The night

I cried, "My father!" in a humiliating meeting of pastors. The unjust charge of building a "church of old ladies". The suffering of being discarded. The accusation of not having the call of God. The shame. My face on the floor. The deep inner wounds. Only the Holy Spirit and I understood that moment.

The altar is my life.

DIPLOMA OF LIFE

I created Universal Church School of Theology as a way of raising pastors, which I started in the old funeral parlor building soon after the opening of the Abolição church. The idea was to have teachers capable of providing a biblical foundation for the first generation of preachers. Many teachers were from other protestant churches, which ended up causing some problems.

Ex-bishop Carlos Rodrigues and the late Bishop Renato Maduro were a part of this academic phase, and influenced by some teachers, began to adopt methods that were different than what we had always learned. One day, a breathless Renato came over to me. He, Rodrigues and the other pastors always gathered at the back of the church after services to talk to God.

On one of these nights, Rodrigues led the prayer with these words:

"Speak Lord *(silence)*… Speak, speak, speak, speak *(silence)*… Speak, Lord *(a longer silence)*…"

He remained motionless, all the pastors holding hands, as if waiting for something to happen. Doubtful, Renato opened one eye and then came looking for me afterwards.

"I don't feel good about the type of prayer that Rodrigues is making. There isn't anything positive about it," he complained, annoyed.

That same day, I gave Rodrigues a stern rebuke and asked him to quit this new custom. He instantly obeyed. Afterwards, he told me that he had learned those things from a Pentecostal course taught by a teacher at our school of theology. It was an attempt to implant the doctrine of prophecy within the Universal Church.

The evil of prophecy, with a shortsighted interpretation of the Protestant church, began to spread at that time. Prophecy, for them, has always been synonymous with fortune-telling. Throughout the years, we have seen countless victims of this religious plague—sincere people deceived by an evil practice. Many have gotten married, changed jobs or moved to another country, or even got divorced, abandoning their children, because a "prophetic pastor" stated that he knew their future.

Look at the practices that God condemned during a harsh rebuke of King Manasseh of Jerusalem: "…used fortune-telling and omens and sorcery, and dealt with mediums and with necromancers. He did much evil in the sight of the Lord, provoking him to anger" (2 Chronicles 33:6, ESV).

What is the difference between a "prophetic pastor" and a fortune-teller that does palm reading?

Nonsense! This makes me nauseous!

And so, in order to avoid importing bad habits from other churches, we decided to close the Universal Church School of Theology. Time has proven that this decision was correct. A course of study in theology does not guarantee the graduation of a good pastor. I have degree after degree, but this does not guarantee my quality as a preacher of the gospel. Of course, knowledge is important, but it does not qualify me as a pastor. I have various diplomas hanging on the wall: Doctor of Christian Philosophy, Master of Theological Science, Doctor of Divinity, and Doctorate of Theology. But I give little importance to these titles.

I use my love of teaching to help directly in the training of pastors. I may have inherited this passion from Rosa and the talents she developed in me. Rosa was a public school teacher who taught me to read and write at Portugal School in São Cristóvão, in Rio.

I used this skill to teach and preach about Christian ideas in public in a hard-hitting, truthful way. I explain how to communicate from the pulpit. I always attempt to use clear examples and simple comparisons, and purposefully use straightforward, unembellished language.

It's my custom to use expressions that are not usually used by anyone else. "Your life is just a pile of manure!" People will immediately think, "Wow, the pastor just called us manure!" This technique prevents people from forgetting the main focus of what is being said, and that's what matters most to me. The Bible itself uses this when God speaks to His people, "… and splatter your faces with manure from your festival sacrifices, and will throw you on the manure pile" (Malachi 2:3). Strong words awaken the belief of those who hear us, I always tell the pastors.

Until now, I have not lost this pleasure of teaching. I feel a satisfaction in passing on what I have learned. I make meetings with my coworkers on the pulpit every week without fail. Above all, I speak about spiritual matters, the main reason for these meetings. There are other meetings as well, normally two or three times a year with bishops that lead the churches in various countries and continents.

These are moments dedicated to total meditation on the Word of God. Many inspirations that helped to transform the lives of thousands of church members have come from these meetings. Primarily, I think about the bishops, pastors, auxiliary pastors and assistants. I value the salvation of each one of them more than the results of any work. I repeat over and over that we should never let down our guard when it comes to spending eternity at God's side. What good is it to gain the whole world and lose your own soul? They know my sincerity, and because of this, they respect me. This is the only way that they can transmit spirit, and not mere biblical information. Passing on this spirit is offering others what you live. It is the giving of faith and life.

I also take special care with the youngest of them. Before becoming pastors, auxiliaries undergo practical training. Most are between the ages of 18 and 25, and are enrolled in the Universal Church Bible Institute. For two or three years they attend meetings and gain experience, then they are sent as auxiliary pastors to a specific church.

I always teach them to see opportunities and not problems. A pastor's spirit has to take charge. I also warn them about the moral and spiritual discipline of the church. Our work is very serious. I teach pastors to be faithful in their conduct and behavior. What spiritual authority does a pastor have to preach the gospel when he has fallen into adultery?

We teach singles and engaged couples how to have good marriages, a fundamental requirement for a pastor's success. But this is not always possible. Some end up marrying by the emotion of the heart. This is one of my main secrets: the building of a solid and happy union by Ester's side, whose confidences will be revealed in Nothing to Lose 3.

We have a department with hundreds of employees throughout Brazil, with the sole purpose of helping pastors. They can learn another language, live in another country, get married, and live a good life. Each pastor receives housing, dental care, a medical plan, and the right to a day off once or twice a week, in addition to a monthly stipend.

I wish I had been given this opportunity.

I am repeatedly asked, "How do you manage such a gigantic organization, with thousands of men and women scattered to every corner of the world? How do you control this army of people? How can you blindly trust those who are isolated from you on the other side of the world? How can you successfully lead a group of people so large?"

The answer is, "The Holy Spirit." There's no other explanation.

What's most common today, both in and outside of Brazil, are pastors who have been trained in prestigious universities, but are ignorant in faith. They're full of knowledge, but devoid of the Holy Spirit. Completely empty of the true genuine belief that transforms those who are in anguish.

My goal has always been to practice the exhortation of the prophet Jeremiah. "And I'll give you shepherds according to My heart, who will feed you with knowledge and understanding" (Jeremiah 3:15). The Universal Church does what other Protestant churches don't, because we combine faith with intelligence. This is the great divide, the great difference between others and us. And because of this, we are role models—wherever we go, the rest will follow.

It's sad to find no leader, neither in nor outside Brazil, interested in saving souls. I say this openly! This is why the majority of Protestants don't like me, or the Universal Church. They have always been among the major obstacles of our growth in various parts of the world. I'm not tied to anyone, and am free to speak the truth. And to do this, I don't need a religious degree or some post-graduate work in theology.

A good pastor is created day-by-day, dealing with the afflicted and needy, in daily sacrifice for lost souls.

The pastors of the Universal Church are not owners of the truth. But the sacrifice that they make on the altar cannot be compared with any other institution. They live without a penny to their name. One day they wake up in the heart of Africa, and on another day they're sleeping in a village along the Amazon River. They take their wives, children if they have them, and a suitcase. Nothing more.

They'll dedicate themselves to work in a beautiful church just as readily as in a church that's no more than a mud hut. They live to help the suffering, always with a smile and a word of faith to uplift the downtrodden. Who truly cares about these people on the fringes, rich or poor, who our pastors embrace? Private institutions? Authorities? Politicians?

Many pastors have not even had the opportunity to bury their own parents in the midst of this spiritual battle. I was one of them. On January 27, 1987, I was unable to go to the city of Juiz de Fora to bury my father, Enrique Francisco Bezerra, as my immigration papers were being processed, which was vital for me to continue preaching in the United States. I have only the memories of a man of integrity and honesty who was a protector of his home.

Even when they had the help of the Church, other pastors and bishops also declined the chance to give final good-byes to their fathers, mothers or other family members, because they were far away, dedicating their lives to the Word of God. This is not insensitivity or lack of love for their families, but absolute surrender of their lives as a sacrifice on the altar.

Before criticizing a pastor of the Universal Church, think about these things.

LETTERS OF HELP

With television programs on TV Tupi during the first three years of the Church's opening, hundreds of letters poured in asking us to open churches in cities all over the country. It was thousands of them a month. We would have loved to open 500 churches all at once in every corner of Brazil, but we didn't have the finances for that, and even more importantly, we didn't have enough trained pastors. We had to take things one step at a time.

We started to spread in Rio de Janeiro, in the neighborhood of Padre Miguel, with a tent-church in a vacant lot behind a supermarket. We didn't even have a concrete floor. I would spend several days a week looking for new properties in Rio, but I also envisioned spreading to other capitals as well. Rio soon had new churches: Grajaú Irajá, Campo Grande, Duque de Caxias, and Nova Iguaçu. Hundreds of pastors and assistants were raised up in these locations over the years, where I personally conducted dozens of meetings and special vigils.

It was time to win over all of Brazil. Beginning in 1979, two years after the first service in the former funeral parlor, we did the same thing in São Paulo and Minas Gerais. The first church outside Rio was opened in the city of Juiz de Fora, and a few days later, I performed the wedding ceremony of Bishop Renato Maduro. He and his wife spent their honeymoon in the mining town of Caxambu, in the same hotel where I had spent my honeymoon with Ester. It was our wedding gift to them.

Days later, I asked Renato to travel to Juiz de Fora to help one of Ester's cousins who was addicted to drugs. Renato had been freed from the same problem after several cocaine overdoses and various rehab clinics.

"Pastor Macedo, this place has potential. There's a lot of suffering in this city," Renato told me by phone.

His excitement made sense. Many young people were enslaved to drugs just like he had been in the past—misery that reached a climax in Juiz de Fora in the late 1970s.

"But there's more, pastor. There's a nightclub that can be rented right in the center of town. It's a sure thing!" he added, referring to "Girafão" (the Big Giraffe), a well known local hangout, where they hosted a loud band Friday to Sunday nights, while the other days of the week the Universal Church began to hold its meetings. This caught the attention of the youth, who began to fill up the deliverance meetings most of all. Many wanted to know firsthand about the amazing story of Renato Maduro.

In the middle of meetings where he would speak about his experiences with drugs, he would talk about salvation in the Lord Jesus. He asked if he could make a flyer with before and after photos of his addiction. These were spread throughout the city, on one side the shocking image of a depressed, long-haired, skeletal Renato, and on the other, a well-dressed, smiling, clean-cut Renato. The meetings packed out. We used the club's sound system, and the deliverance prayers were made in the middle of the dance floor, with a disco ball and spotlights hanging from the ceiling.

Some months later, the club began to empty out and the owner offered to lease the full property to us—I agreed on the spot. We bought some time on a local radio station and the church immediately grew. I even made several meetings there. Today we have 22 churches in the region of Juiz de Fora, and more than 600 in the state of Minas Gerais.

Around the same time in São Paulo, the first Universal Church was opened in an old building on Avenida Doutor Gentil de Moura, in the Ipiranga neighborhood, a busy area of the city. The room was hot. Meetings were sweltering during the day and infested with flies at night. Later, we moved to a church in the popular neighborhood of Parque Dom Pedro, a hub for busses coming from different parts of the capital, and then to a bankrupt movie theater on Celso Garcia Avenue, a few blocks away from where the Temple of Solomon is being built today.

While all this was happening, I made many meetings in rented theaters in the state of São Paulo. Affiliates of TV Tupi had good coverage throughout the state, which allowed us to organize crowded events in Campinas, Sorocaba, Ribeirão Preto and other regions. In Rio, we copied this strategy. Many cinemas showed pornographic movies on certain days of the week, and our work of faith was held in the same cinemas on the remaining days. Cine Bruni, in Meier and Praça Tiradentes were two examples of this. In Copacabana, the former Cine Alaska was the same. Many of these theaters were later transformed into regional headquarters of the Universal Church.

The following year, we set out for Bahia. I was in the mother church, Abolição, thinking about which of our pastors was best suited for this important mission. Salvador (the capital) would be the Universal Church's gateway to the entire Northeast. Later, I parked in front of the Grajaú church in Rio, where Pastor Paulo Roberto Guimarães had taken his first steps as a preacher.

"Paulo, do you have faith to go to Salvador and open our church there?" I asked bluntly.

"Yes, I do. I want to serve God," he replied in the same manner.

The change was quick. A few days later, after being married for less than a month, Paulo Roberto stepped out onto Rua do Tijolo, in Praça de Sé, the traditional neighborhood of Bahia, near Elevador Lacerda, where we had already rented some space. The small room had been used to store garbage in the basement of a building called Themis.

The area was the epitome of urban decay. Prostitutes, transvestites, drug addicts and drug dealers fought each other day and night. Drunks urinated on the steps leading to our meeting room, giving the place a terrible smell. Close by two waste containers attracted mosquitoes, cockroaches and even rats. To make matters worse, the church had no windows or ventilation of any type.

Paulo Roberto remembers that he was shocked and could not believe his eyes when he first saw that place. The thought that he would be unable to convince people to give the church a try even crossed his mind. This was a traumatic experience for someone so young—he was 20.

The following week my home phone rang.

"Pastor Macedo, this place we rented isn't going to work. It's really bad—the worst in Salvador. It's a garbage dump!" he told me, followed by a long, detailed description of the devastating scene.

I allowed Paulo Roberto to let it all out, then answered him quickly:

"Praise God, Paulo! That's the perfect place. That's where the Universal Church is going to explode. Those people need the Gospel more than anyone else—suffering people that need a change of life!"

Paulo Roberto remembers this conversation until today:

"At that moment I understood the real dimension of the Work of God. I simply believed and obeyed. I hung up the phone and started to view that place in a different way. It was the place that God had chosen to transform lives like never before in Bahia."

On the afternoon of July 20, 1980, we opened our first church in the Northeast and had one thousand people. The hall had a capacity for 250 plastic chairs. Many people were outside. The crowd filled up a parking lot next to the church, and had come because of invitations we had made on the TV Tupi affiliates. In addition, we had handed out flyers and put up posters for several weeks in Salvador.

Days after the opening, we were forced to have five meetings a day to meet the demand. The majority would attend meetings on their feet. There was one bathroom for both men and women, and the lack of ventilation made the Bahian heat even more unbearable. Even so, in the middle of chaos, many people were freed from their sordid pasts and gained the riches of a new birth.

Today Bahia has more than 540 churches, 16,000 assistants and countless members. In the Northeast region of the country, we have more than 2,000 churches.

A year after our arrival in Salvador, in an August 1981 *Plenitude* (magazine of the Church) interview, I commented on our projects and my intentions to spread the Church to every corner of the country. The number of requests for churches that were sent to our TV programs multiplied. Here's an excerpt from the interview:

Reporter: *"Has the Universal Church achieved your goals for Brazil?"*

Bishop Macedo: *"No. There is still a lot to do. We plan to have a nationwide TV program by July, and by the end of this year, we plan to have at least one church in each state of Brazil."*

Reporter: *"Does the Universal Church have the money for these projects?"*

Bishop Macedo: *"Actually, no. But we have faith, and that's the most important of all. People always help when they recognize that a work is from God. If false religions and cults grow and spread throughout the world, why can't a work of God, with the anointing of the Holy Spirit, do the same?"*

Later you will become familiar with the unmatched growth of the Universal Church throughout the rest of Brazil, but first you need to hear about how a never-before-seen war arose in Brazil. A battle against hell that Brazilians had never witnessed.

Evil was about to be unmasked.

YES, DEMONS DO EXIST

The great majority of requests for new churches were motivated by one thing: they wanted deliverance. Brazil was in the middle of an extreme worship of symbols and spirits. It was common for people to wear a guide (symbol of a spirit guide) or an amulet around their necks, or to place offerings to spirits at waterfalls, intersections or cemeteries. The pleas for help intensified. At times I spent hours reading the letters.

I think this was one of the principal revelations from God in the trajectory of the Universal Church: develop a fierce, direct strategy for confronting evil like no other institution in the world has ever done. The Book of Acts draws an exact picture of this work of the Universal Church: "… how God anointed Jesus of Nazareth with the Holy Spirit and with power, who went about doing good and healing all who were oppressed by the devil, for God was with Him" (Acts 10:38).

The devil, demons and hell do exist, and act against people today just like they acted in the past, and will continue to act in the future. They were not invented by me nor by the Universal Church. Clear and obvious references about them are available to any reader of the Bible.

The quotes are so transparent that they leave no doubt, and are scattered throughout the Old and New Testaments.

I selected seven short passages for you to reflect upon in a deep, unbiased manner. Read them for what they are, and come to your own conclusion.

The song of Moses

"They sacrificed to demons, not to God, to gods they did not know, to new gods, new arrivals…"

(Deuteronomy 32:17)

God's conversation with Satan

"Then the LORD said to Satan, 'Have you considered My servant Job, that there is none like him on the earth, a blameless and upright man, one who fears God and shuns evil?' So Satan answered the LORD and said, 'Does Job fear God for nothing?'"

(Job 1:8,9)

Supplication of David

"The wicked shall be turned into hell, and all the nations that forget God."

(Psalm 9:17)

The discovery of the apostles

"Then the seventy returned with joy, saying, 'Lord, even

the demons are subject to us in Your name!'"

(Luke 10:17)

From the lips of Jesus

"When an unclean spirit goes out of a man, he goes through dry places, seeking rest, and finds none. Then he says, 'I will return to my house from which I came.' And when he comes, he finds it empty, swept, and put in order. Then he goes and takes with him seven other spirits more wicked than himself, and they enter and dwell there; and the last state of that man is worse than the first. So shall it also be with this wicked generation."

(Matthew 12:43-45)

Teaching of the Apostle Paul

"Put on the whole armor of God, that you may be able to stand against the wiles of the devil."

(Ephesians 6:11)

The revelation of the Apocalypse

"The devil, who deceived them, was cast into the lake of fire and brimstone where the beast and the false prophet are. And they will be tormented day and night forever and ever."

(Revelation 20:10)

Still a young pastor, at the very beginning of my life on the altar, I drew my own conclusions.

I decided that the Universal Church would rise up against evil as had never happened before. Courage would be demanded, determination, and above all, the guidance of the Holy Spirit. I had been called for this. It wouldn't matter if people accused me of brainwashing or mind control. These spirits were the source of evil and this needed to be announced in a candid, straightforward manner.

They kill, steal and destroy by working in the inner core of people. I myself had been held hostage by evil. As a young man I suffered through unsuccessful attempts at healing a disease of my skin. A cross was drawn on my body at a "spiritual energy center" known as Santo Antônio de Pádua. But my condition worsened. I did not manifest (the experience of having an evil spirit possess or take over the conscious functioning of your body for a time), but demons were working in my life. The Protestant church where Ester and I had been "born" did not believe in confronting evil spirits directly.

Believers have always been afraid of demons. Pastors would avoid the subject. No church was willing to get in the gutter to help millions of Brazilians who were lost in darkness. That bothered me, shook me to the core. After meditating on the words of Jesus, I understood the authority that was given to true Christians, "Behold, I give you the authority to trample on serpents and scorpions, and over all the power of the enemy, and nothing shall by any means hurt you" (Luke 10:19).

I decided to show who was who. I would call the spirits by name and expose them in front of everyone, and fearlessly attack them with all my strength. Making a distinction was necessary: the good and the bad, the strong and the weak, the children of light and the children of darkness, God and the devil.

My dream was to invade hell and rescue souls. This desire pulsed through my veins. Nothing and no one could stop me. Absolutely nothing could cause me harm. That was a promise. It was the time to prove the truth of my belief in God and in His calling on my life. Either He was real or He wasn't. Either the Bible was true, God existed and was with me, or everything I had believed in was a farce. How could I know this?

I began to challenge the spirits.

The first declaration of war happened during our program on Radio Metropolitana that had inherited an audience of a famous psychic. Live, on the air, I called my listeners to come to church and witness a showdown of faith (literally, a clash of gods). The God of the Universal Church against the spirits that caused sickness, and the symptoms of possession, who the psychic before us had called "evolved angels" and "guardian angels."

"I want to see how strong your spirit is! Bring your spirit to the church so everyone can see who is stronger! My God, or your guide!" I announced confrontationally to the call-in listeners over the radio.

I received many threats. They'd say that the spirits would kill me or break my legs during the meeting as everyone watched. When the people who came to challenge God arrived at the church, they would collapse on the floor, possessed by demons.

Rio de Janeiro was infested with offerings laid out for the gods and spirits of witchcraft, which took up enormous amounts of space from cemetery sidewalks on the outskirts of town to the busy streets of upscale neighborhoods. There were constant reports of animals and even children that were taken and sacrificed to these spirits, but hardly ever was anyone punished for this. Record Network was not yet ours. We couldn't use it to expose such extreme depravity.

One of the most striking cases for me during those years was that of a young man from Rio who would eat the remains of bodies as a part of witchcraft rituals done in the cemetery. The man had sworn to kill me, and was determined to do so with what is known as "the evil eye". Because of this, he had surrendered himself to these spirits. The spirits that he had bowed down to fell to their knees; these forces that had possessed his body mind and soul were unmasked in front of almost 2,000 people.

Upon his deliverance from these spirits, he began to tell us his story over our program for more than a week. I was sued for doing this over Radio Metropolitana, but was cleared by the courts. Another young victim of similar rituals appeared in the church with a body covered in small blisters. During the deliverance prayers, the wounds bled so much that I was covered from head to toe.

The strategy of confronting evil was taken to our television programs on TV Tupi. Soon our churches were packed with people, desperate to get rid of the cruel torment of these spirits. Even pastors from other churches sent their members to the Universal Church for deliverance. This still happens today.

Our Friday meetings in Abolição were packed to over-flowing. We chose Fridays for the chain of deliverance because it was a day when the worst forms of witchcraft were, and still are, practiced. This inspiration came from the teaching of the Lord Jesus, "You shall know the truth, and the truth shall make you free" (John 8:32).

One Friday morning, as I was preaching in the old funeral parlor, one of the head witchdoctors silently came into the church. He sat in the back and glared at me. Agostinho Ignácio da Silva was 41 years old, and as a young man, had immersed himself in this dark world after some witchcraft had been done between himself and his ex-girlfriend.

In a consultation with a witchdoctor, he'd been told to develop his psychic ability. He was a young black man, stocky with a stern face, who had served these spirits for more than 20 years. He held many consultations in his own house, which grew to a following of hundreds of people. The spirits would decide even what he wore and ate each day. No one had ever laid their hands on his head. He had had intercourse with the spirits in the body of an imaginary woman.

"You who have, or have had any involvement with spirits, come up to the altar and close your eyes now," I gave the invitation over the microphone.

Agostinho stayed where he was and just watched. The prayer began and all of a sudden, within a few seconds, a scream echoed through the church. A spirit had manifested in his body. From a distance, I ordered those spirits to bring this burly man up to the altar where I was standing.

With arms crossed behind him, fingers forcefully contorted, and his head bent forward, Agostinho was a fearful sight coming towards me. He charged forward like a wild bull. It looked like he would slam his head against the altar, when suddenly, just a few inches away, the spirit stopped him. Had the spirits succeeded, it would have been a great tragedy.

He argued and screamed ferociously. Afterwards, in agreement with all the pastors and assistants, I affirmed his complete freedom. This was the first and only time that Agostinho manifested evil spirits after walking through our doors.

From then on, he became my smiling, cheerful consultant so that I could better understand the work of evil spirits. I interviewed him various times and told his story of change over the radio and television programs, clearing up doubts and bringing awareness of the truth to many people.

In the early 1980s, with his help, I related my experiences in my controversial book called, "Orixás, Caboclos and Guides: Gods or Demons" which was officially launched at an event in a stadium called Maracanãzinho. The book was published in Portuguese, English and Spanish. In one of the more recent editions, the cover had an illustration of a burning candle that appeared to swell to the point of bursting and was advertised on the main TV stations in Brazil.

The book, which had been censored for a time, simply tells the truth about the harmful effects of evil spirits.

EYES FILLED
WITH OPPRESSION

People possessed with the most varied and sinister evil came through the doors of the Universal Church. Each person had a dramatic story of demon possession. Symptoms were painful. They heard voices and saw shadows, had wounds all over their bodies, constant fainting spells, extreme mood swings, insomnia and headaches with no medical explanation; they were victims of all types of physical and emotional illnesses.

With the great demand for deliverance meetings, I decided to start midnight vigils on Fridays. These were powerful meetings set on the day and time that the worst witchcraft was done throughout Brazil. People came from all over Rio and stood for hours to join in the overcrowded meetings.

The walls of Abolição dripped with sweat from the enormous amount of heat generated by all the people there.

Tania, the widow of Bp. Renato Maduro, had been personally counseled by me. The first prayer I made for her, I placed my hands on her head and called forth the chief spirit that worked in her and in her then boyfriend.

"I blacked out. I don't remember anything from that moment. When I came to, I asked what had happened. This happened even though I had been a Catholic and had never stepped foot into a place that practiced witchcraft," she remembers.

The battle against demons was grueling. One time, the spirit in the body of Tania lifted an entire church pew over her head, difficult for someone of her small stature. With an altered voiced, the evil spirit recounted everything it had done in their lives. Before the meeting, on a national day that celebrates spirits that "protect" children, Tania had had an argument with Renato, and full of hatred, she dug her nails into his neck. When the meeting ended, she came to my office as I was getting ready to leave.

"Is everything okay, Tania?" I asked, seeing the oppression in her eyes.

"No, it's not okay, she said," explaining how she had reacted that day in anger. "My hands are in a cold sweat. Look how it's dripping off my hands."

No sooner had she finished speaking than I jumped over the table, pushed a chair out of the way and ordered the demon that was causing this trouble to manifest. The spirit immediately began to shout. At other times, I would usually have to immobilize her arms and stop her from hitting her head on the floor. Tania went through an intense process of deliverance until she totally surrendered her life on the altar. And this is how she and thousands of other assistants, pastors, pastors' wives and bishops have in the end been able to turn around and help us rescue other victims of evil.

A very common sight was that of desperate mothers with their babies convulsing with a high fever. One night, a mother brought in her child that was almost unconscious. Tania was the first to greet the poor distraught woman.

"Pastor, she's fainting. I've already taken her to five different hospitals and emergency rooms. No one can understand why she has this fever, said the mother in tears, just a short time before the midnight vigil. She's only eight months old. For the love of God, help me!"

I acted decisively.

"Tania, take the baby and go out to the street right now!"

I determined that the evil spirit working in the child would manifest in the mother at that very moment. The demon revealed itself and was cast out by the power of the name of the Lord Jesus.

"I took the baby to the sidewalk in my arms, unconscious and burning with fever. When I came back into the church after the prayer, she was fine. Seeing that little baby healed, I understood what happiness at home was," recounts Tania.

My challenges continued on radio and TV and our meetings were packed out. I decided to hold special meetings called, The Chain of the White Table. Never had so many people come at once. Most people wanted to personally see the battle between the God of the Universal Church and the god of the famous Dr. Fritz.

It was a time when many people sought out the help of what was called "spiritual surgery" in the Bonsucesso neighborhood of Rio. He charged for each "surgery" that he performed, as well as for parking spaces, and would rent out chairs for those who waited in line. I asked in the church why Dr. Fritz was not called Dr. Joe or Dr. John.

"Is it because a German name gives the connotation of an evolved race?" I questioned, as I ordered evil spirits that worked in the body of Dr. Fritz to manifest.

"Here the Lord Jesus truly does invisible operations."

Some years later, this "doctor" attempted suicide and was taken to court for various crimes, including the illegal practice of medicine, bodily injury, murder, and denying aid to someone in distress.

Our audacious assault on these spirits, coincidence or not, brought about serious consequences. One Sunday afternoon, Ester was a victim of a kidnapping. Through the window, Cristiane noticed that her mother drove home and parked on the street, and sped off again in the company of three men. Ester was assaulted and dragged into the car.

"They knew who I was. One of them said, 'Put your head down, we're passing in front of your husband's church,'" remembers Ester, which makes us doubt that this was a random criminal act.

It was agonizing. I went out to the street, desperately searching for Ester. At that time, there were no cell phones. After searching the neighborhood for hours, I returned home and finally found her. We cried in each other's arms. That was the first time that Cristiane had seen her mother weeping aside from times of prayer.

It was also the first time that Ester had seen a weapon up close. She had been freed by the criminals just a few blocks away from where she had been taken. They had kept their pistol pointed at her until they crossed a quiet street, when a group of teenagers noticed something strange about the car. The kidnappers got scared and ordered Ester out without looking back.

God delivered our family one more time.

The experience changed my way of thinking. In a state of shock from this violent attack at home, and the constant threats from those who worshiped the spirits, I decided to start carrying a gun. I would carry a .38 caliber pistol and many times hid it in the pulpit as I was preaching on the altar. Later, as I was writing the book, "In the Footsteps of Jesus", the Holy Spirit touched me and convicted me that carrying a weapon was a lack of trust in Him. Immediately I made a vow and said, "Today onwards, I will never carry a weapon. But Lord, if you don't protect my life and my family, I'm going to buy a machine gun." As I always say, I'm not in favor of carrying weapons. I always advise church members not to react to a robbery or any other kind of violence.

In spite of all the threats, I continued on in my commitment to preach the truth. God saw the honesty of my intentions.

One of the most memorable midnight vigils in Abolição happened on Good Friday, 1983. A girl came up on the altar, possessed by a demon, led there by one of our pastors. As usual, I told the spirit to get on its knees and told it to speak about the evil it was causing in the girl's life. She was unhappy in her love life and had an uncontrollable addiction to cocaine and marijuana.

Without thinking, I asked about a subject that had dominated the news that week. A famous Brazilian singer known for songs that extolled the virtues of witchcraft was in the hospital after a routine surgery in Rio and hanging between life and death.

"Demons, what are you doing in her body?" I asked before a packed church.

The manifesting spirits answered my question:

"I'm the one that's there! I won't let her die and I won't let her live... She's not doing what's right. I'm going to drag out her suffering. I'm the one that's there!"

I ordered the demon to be quiet and commanded all the other spirits that were working in the body of that woman in the hospital to come. Then together with the church members, we set the young woman free. Then, I said:

"Listen people... Either this singer will die, or she's going to wake up. But she's going to leave that hospital," I declared, using authority in the name of Jesus.

Hours later, the news came: The singer died in the early hours between Good Friday and Saturday.

SPIRIT AGAINST SPIRIT

I was in the habit of inviting anyone who doubted the existence of satanic spirits, to come up to the altar. That has always been a way for people to prove to themselves the reality of these demons. Few had the courage to do it. One day, in the city of Itu, a man accepted my offer in front of 15,000 who were gathered in the stadium of Dr. Novelli Junior.

"A lot of people are just full of hot air. Right now I challenge any doctor, psychiatrist or psychic to prove that this manifestation here is a lie," I prodded, pointing to a young woman who was manifesting demons. "If anyone wants to, I'll allow them to make a test."

A middle-aged man came to the stage that had been set up on the field and courageously interrupted me. I asked if he was a head spiritist. After that, there was a heated exchange between us.

"If you doubt this, then, show me what you've got," I said.

"Let's go," calling me to come with him to the place where he practiced spiritism.

"This is a soccer field, a neutral location," he snapped.

The crowd started to boo, and I goaded him on even further.

"Are you afraid of being bitten?"

"I'm not afraid. I just want to know the name of this spirit, but I'm not afraid," the man replied.

"Well, if you think it's a lie, come up here and make your test. Are you afraid? Come up here!"

With the possessed woman in hand, I took some steps towards the fearless man. He began to talk to her.

"If you're a spirit like mine, why don't you come here to me?"

The spirit in the woman just glared at him.

"Why don't you come into me, come here! Come into me, come into me, come into me!" he insisted.

There was no reaction in the man, so I decided to ignore him and continue the meeting together with the people. We set the possessed woman free from the spirit that had contorted her entire body. All of a sudden, while we were casting out the evil from the remaining people who were manifesting, the man who had stopped challenging me lost it.

Several pastors tried to control him, but he kept on arguing with an uncommon force. The more we prayed, the more he insulted us, and the more I used my faith. During deliverance, the more a demon reacts, the more forcefully we want to react back.

After a few minutes of manifesting, he was set free and I hugged him as the people applauded.

I came across this man 24 years later in December 2011 during an Internet broadcast of IURDTV, streamed live from the São Paulo church in the neighborhood of Santo Amaro. He told me that he had continued to be addicted to drugs, that he was sorry and was looking for help in the church. We laid our hands on him and prayed, and once again he manifested other evil spirits. After commanding his deliverance, I asked:

"What's going on inside of you right now?"

"Relief. I feel light. It's like I'm in the clouds," he responded and smiled.

The case of this man from Itu raises the question that many people have asked during the four decades of the Universal Church: What's the secret to a complete and final deliverance?

There is only one path: sincerity and sacrifice. Sincerity to confess, to wholeheartedly repent and to tear out the hidden sins from inside of you. The Lord Jesus erases your sins and forgives you at that instant. And then, sacrifice to go on from there, to immediately abandon your old life that had been far from God.

The Universal Church is for sincere people. It's not for hypocrites who are a product of religiosity. It's for honest people, in search of a way out. A prostitute can be in bed, selling herself, carried along by the misfortunes of life, but crying out within, "I don't want this for my life! My God, show me a way out, take me out of this!" We will go in to hell itself to help these kinds of people.

Since the phase of Abolição, I've come across a more efficient way to awaken people's faith. Many times I could not understand why I preached and prayed so much, yet people still didn't receive the miracle they needed. Of course the Bible has an answer for everything. For days I reflected on the time the Lord Jesus used only one word to heal people, "When evening had come, they brought to Him many who were demon-possessed, and He cast out the spirits with a word, and healed all who were sick" (Matthew 8:16).

In other situations, there were special ways to bring about healing, as happened in Galilee. "Then they brought to Him one who was deaf and had an impediment in his speech, and they begged Him to put His hand on him. And He took him aside from the multitude, and put His fingers in his ears, and He spat and touched his tongue. Then looking up to heaven, He sighed, and said to him, 'Ephphatha,' that is, 'Be opened.' Immediately his ears were opened, and the impediment of his tongue was loosed, and he spoke plainly" (Mark 7:32-35).

While meditating on these passages, I questioned the need for Jesus to put His fingers in his ears and saliva on the tongue to heal the deaf-mute man. Why didn't He just use one word to heal him?

Together with my day-to-day experiences in the church, I concluded that there are people who can only be freed when, for example, they are anointed on the area of their infirmities, or they take a blessed rose to their house, or salt to sprinkle in their business or even to drink a cup of pure water.

The idea of deliverance and the use of biblical symbols to awaken people's faith have brought multitudes to the Universal Church.

The incredible growth of the church has incurred a high cost to my personal life.

SO FAR, AND YET SO CLOSE

The early years of total dedication to the church consumed almost all my family time. This was one of the prices I had to pay for placing my present and future on the altar.

I confess I hardly saw my two beloved daughters as they were growing up. My involvement in rescuing lost souls was so great that it forced me to give up leisure time alongside my girls. After the adoption of Moses, and our departure to the United States, I was closer to my children.

Ester, always a wise woman of God, played a key role in the home to make up for my absence. In the early years of Abolição, whenever I thought of enjoying a few hours with Cristiane and Viviane, I was always called away by some responsibility or activity of the church, a mission trip or some kind of last-minute spiritual emergency. Our growth demanded everything from me. I am aware that I was an absent father, and yet at no time has this ever diminished my great love for my children.

Thank God they did not grow up rebellious. On the contrary, Cristiane and Viviane chose to follow the same path of self-denial as their father, of their own free will. This gladdens my heart. Both are wives of successful bishops in their roles in the church.

Nearly four decades later, every once in a while I speak openly with Cristiane and Viviane about that phase of our lives. In fact, for much of their childhood, they did not know their father closely. As they relive all that I went through, in the name of a higher cause—our faith—they are able to understand what was going on.

I gave up the pleasure of being close to my little girls, for the belief that I held within me. What other father would give this up?

Not that what I did was right or wrong, but I was driven by a greater cause. The Spirit of God led me. Today it comforts me to know what Cristiane thinks. She had a different childhood; she was forced to accept the fact that her parents' attention was focused on her younger sister, the victim of a serious health problem from the moment she came into this world. We were fighting against a disease that triggered the birth of the Universal Church of the Kingdom of God.

In the preparations for this book, I received letters from Cristiane and Viviane with touching disclosures, written especially for me.

These letters have never been made public.

They speak directly about me as a father, unconditional love and gratitude for their mother, and reveal something special to me. These words make me stronger today. Cristiane and Viviane understand the values that made me act the way I did, simply because they now have the same spirit as their father.

I am pleased to share two letters with whoever reads this book. The following words are from Cristiane:

Dear Dad,

We often speak about how we got to know each other better in my teens, when the circumstances of our move to New York made it possible for us to spend more time together, but rarely do we talk about the dad we knew before this... a dad unlike so many others.

I grew up in a happy family, though quite different from the happy family that's normally idealized, where the father plays with his daughter, the family spends time together, children participate in school activities and are prepared for a career and a promising future.

Vivi and her constant surgeries removed me from the center of attention when I was only one year old. Then I developed asthma, which made me so weak on cloudy days.

You both worked so hard that the hours that you had at home were for resting. Almost nothing was left for us. And so, our life was different from other families.

We had no plans for the future and changed schools six times in rapid succession. We didn't take vacations, we didn't go to parties and didn't have a social life. It was home to school, school to home, home to church, church to home.

I learned to play on the carpet and have my sister as my best and only friend.

For those who don't understand what true happiness is, our childhood does sound dull, but it wasn't, even though all the components were there. Do you know why? Because I didn't need to be the center of attention to feel valued.

I didn't need to be physically strong to feel capable.

I didn't need your attention to know how much you loved me.

I didn't need vacations to enjoy life.

I didn't need a social life to know true friendship.

I didn't need a career to be who I am today.

Dad, you gave me everything I needed. And all this came, not because of what you couldn't give me, but because of who you were and continue to be: a man of faith.

Your absence from the house was never motivated by an absence in our lives.

We had a father who was faithful to our mother, who loved his family to the point that he protected us from what was not good, a father who taught us the principles of faith, the value of family, who had a love, not of words, but by example.

We went to bed early, didn't watch soap operas, didn't go over to classmates' houses, and because of this, grew up in a home that was pure and full of respect. You might not have always been there, but when you were, you were loving and made us feel like true princesses.

How many times did I have an asthma attack and could only sleep between the two of you, but you never complained or grumbled. When I woke up in the middle of the night, you'd be asleep on the floor so that I could sleep well next to Mom.

Since the beginning our goal has always been the same: battle evil with all of our strength. The book *Orixás, caboclos e guias* opened the eyes of many people.

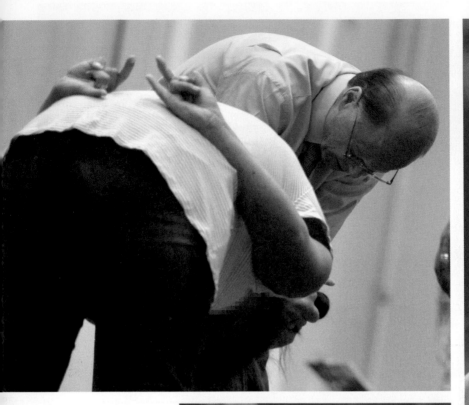

A moment of faith and joy. After fighting for the spiritual freedom of a member, I was given a touching hug of thanks.

After plazas and cinemas, I decided to be bold. The first was the Olaria Gymnasium. We made meetings in Maracanãzinho and Maracanã, in Rio, in order to bring the Holy Spirit to people who were in anguish, and thirsty for faith.

JESUS CRISTO
É O SENHOR

Convoys from all
over Brazil braved
the intense heat of
the Rio summer.
Over 250 thousand
worshipers turned
Maracanã into an
enormous Universal
Church.

In April of 2010, an event entitled "D-Day" broke all attendance records for outdoor meetings: only in Botafogo Bay, in Rio, 2 million people were united in the same faith. An image for the history books.

Multitudes in Brazil: São Paulo also gathered 2 million people at the Interlagos Formula 1 racetrack. In total, more than 8 million came together in huge, simultaneous outdoor meetings around the country.

PARANÁ

MINAS GERAIS

A tragedy in our path:
the collapse of the church
in Osasco, São Paulo, in
September 1998. I mourned
with each victim. From that
day on we began church
construction projects
throughout Brazil and around
the world.

Telhado de templo cai e mata 28

The new church in Osasco opened some years after the fatalities that scarred our lives.

The answer of God: large churches built to provide comfort and security represented a turning point in the history of the Universal Church.

MINAS GERAIS

CEARÁ

PARAÍBA

A meeting in the church of Santo Amaro, São Paulo; the pleasure of teaching the gospel continues to pulse in my veins.

These are the big small things that make for a happy family. It's not what you give a family or what you do for them, but who you are.

Father, you are a father who was able to represent God in the right way to his children. Today I am happy because I know this God that you demonstrated to me from my first day of life.

My father, my example—I always respected you and the more time passes, the more reason I have to admire and honor you for the honor and glory of the Lord Jesus.

I love you,
Cris

Now, a never-before-revealed letter by Viviane. Another special moment experienced by a father of 68.

Dear Daddy,
I remember my childhood so well. How good it was to be surrounded by my family, without knowing that it was giving me all the help and support that I would need to face and live in the world.

You were not always with us, but you never gave me a reason to be rebellious. In the few times that you were present, you were loving, and gave me what I needed.

Why do I say this?

I wanted a lot of attention. I wanted to be the favorite at home, to fill the absence of attention that I felt from other people.

I was disciplined innumerable times by Mom for being angry inside for not being accepted at school and elsewhere. But that discipline gave me the assurance that I was not alone, that I had someone fighting for me. Along with this, Mom was always very careful, present and loving. Her zeal was obvious.

Many times I noted your agony when I was disciplined by Mom. This captivated me and made me love you more.

I saw a father who could see my soul, my pain, my agony and feel so cut up by my defects. You were always there, present with words of comfort.

You were not only a pastor at church, but at home.

You backed up your words. They had spirit and life. You saw my soul, even though I was just a child. You gave me what I needed.

I wonder: how could you see things inside of me that I didn't even tell you about? How were you able to say what I needed to hear? How were you able to meet my needs when we had so little time together? How, if I never shared my struggles?

I was very closed off to what was inside of me. I didn't know that I had the opportunity and the power to free myself. This is the pastor that I am talking about. You were the pastor of my soul. You did exactly what you were doing in the church. You met my need and guided me by example.

I loved you without knowing how to express it. Showering you with kisses the few times that we were together was the only way I knew how to express it. But I never knew how to talk about what was happening with me.

You know God because you see through the eyes of a soul in need, and because of that, you have eyes to see other souls. You gave me what the world and your time could not give—salvation to an afflicted soul.

And because of this, I love you more than you can imagine.

Today I see what I have become. I am the result of a couple living in tune with God, who taught me to be balanced, disciplined, and above all, happy.

Father, thank you for seeing my soul.

I loved and love you, because I see you as my role model. I understand all that you did and are ready to do, because you were always the same—someone who loves souls!

Kisses,

Vivi

GODLY MOTHERHOOD

An endless multitude came together to watch the first show of a rock band in an open stadium. The Beatles were a worldwide phenomenon. Shea Stadium in New York in the US had a record attendance of over 55,000 fans for the English band. The scenes of the concert in August 1965 did not leave my memory for years. I was only 20 years old and had just gone through the most important moments of my life: my encounter with God.

The images created a constant indignation inside of me. "How could a rock band gather so many people, while churches have a handful of two or three hundred? They only offer emotion and momentary happiness. It's not right that a meeting of faith that rescues the suffering can't bring in the same or more. God is great and needs to show that no one is greater than Him."

This desire haunted me for the first years after our church had begun, until I had the courage to rent the Olaria

Gymnasium in Rio in order to make the first big meeting of the Universal Church. It worked. More than 7,000 people filled the chairs of the arena. Most continued on as faithful members of the church.

The path was open.

On this very day, Viviane was going through health problems. She was about to turn four and she still had the aftereffects of a serious infection on her cleft lip. Her wounds went from her tongue to her esophagus, according to her doctors.

"Many times it seemed like she was going to die. She was unable to eat anything or even drink milk," remembers Ester, as if she was replaying a movie in her memory.

We came back from the doctor on Friday, and on Saturday afternoon, deep in thought and tense, I left home for the Olaria Gymnasium, with my child screaming in pain.

"Take care of Viviane, Ester. A lot of suffering people are waiting for this meeting. The Lord will protect our home. He sees our sacrifice," I said as I left.

Nothing would stop me. My covenant was with God.

After the town squares and cinemas, we decided to be daring. We wanted to do something remarkable to attract those who were suffering and thirsty for the faith taught by the Universal Church. I was certain that we could help and reconstruct an even greater number of lives.

In September 1980, in the Abolição headquarters, we made another decisive step. We decided to organize the first big meeting in the Maracanãzinho Gymnasium. At that time, only the Brazilian national volleyball team or renowned artists could fill the seats.

I accepted this challenge. I gathered the pastors and shared this goal with the team.

"Listen! Let's fill Maracanãzinho. Who has faith to join me?" I asked, followed by the enthusiasm of the other preachers.

We invited the members of our other churches to the largest deliverance meeting ever made in Brazil. A wide range of distinct religions that had never heard of the Universal Church saw the concrete results of this work. I happily walked up on the stage with a simple wooden pulpit that Sunday afternoon. More than 30,000 packed the gymnasium. It was a day that marked my life and the life of anyone who had the privilege to join in this memorable moment.

The march onward intensified. In the following years, we filled the small soccer stadium of Bangu and organized two or more annual meetings in Maracanãzinho. In November of 1984, in another major event in the largest gymnasium in Rio, I announced a fast with the goal of seeing our participants receive the baptism in the Holy Spirit.

Interestingly, without knowing, three of our main bishops today were there on that day. Romualdo Panceiro, Clodomir Santos and Sérgio Corrêa, each one confronting their own struggles, all had an unforgettable experience with God that Saturday afternoon.

"The spiritual indignation of Bishop grabbed my attention. How could he speak that way to God? What kind of authority was this? I wanted this boundless conviction to change my life," remembers Romualdo, 17 at the time, who had an encounter with God.

"The truth conveyed in his words shook me to the core. I was empty, incomplete, lost, but with a burning desire to find a way out. I wanted God inside of me," agrees Clodomir, who was also baptized in the Holy Spirit.

The previous week, on the radio, we declared a seven-day fast for each participant to empty themselves spiritually. To deny their own desires in order to obey the teachings of the gospel. Before and after work, going to or coming back from any appointment, the agreement was to get on our knees on the altar of Abolição for a few minutes at a time, and ask for a new life.

The joining of our efforts caused the Holy Spirit to breathe on us, and created men and women who were used by God to destroy the artillery of hell all over the world.

What splendid memories!

From there on out, our vision began to focus on a more challenging goal: Maracanã. At the time, it was the largest stadium in the world. Maracanãzinho could no longer contain our numbers. I knew that we already had the ability for this test of courage.

God would honor us.

The obstacles were political. In one of our last meetings in that gymnasium in May of 1986, I sent a message directly to the persecutors of the Universal Church.

"For some years now, Maracanãzinho has been too small for our meetings. Many tell me, 'Bishop Macedo, I would love this meeting to be in Maracanã.' Me too, immensely.

We don't want anything for free. We will pay, but even so, they will put a thousand restrictions in our way because we don't depend on politics. I'm sorry. Next year, the politicians will change, and our situations will also change. We will be in Maracanã," I announced over the gymnasium sound system.

The previous year, a new governor had been elected for Rio de Janeiro. Leonel Brizola left his position to Moreira Franco. Then, in April 1987, the year that the Universal Church had been in existence for one decade, was the most unforgettable period of all of our large meetings.

For the first time, Maracanã would be filled by a people more faithful and zealous than any soccer club. Good Friday, a holiday heavy with religious tradition in Brazil, was chosen for the legendary "Showdown of Faith". The name had a strategic objective: to stimulate the faith of those who wanted to see a confrontation between the God of the Universal Church and the gods of this world.

That's what happened. More than 200,000 people filled the stands of Maracanã, three hours before the event began. Many families arrived after the gates had already been closed. Cars and convoys of busses were lined up in the parking lots.

"I traveled hour after hour from Sao Paulo. We left the night before, leading a group from the church. We faced the sweltering Rio heat with a contagious faith," recounts Bishop Renato Cardoso, my son-in-law, an assistant at that time.

"My mother took me. I was so full of evil spirits that I slept the whole time and only woke up when Bishop ended the meeting. Before leaving, I was given a songbook by an assistant. That was a seed. The Holy Spirit would use Bishop to completely transform me," remembers Guaracy Santos, today the bishop responsible for holding showdowns of faith that still take place around the world.

Never before had any religious movement been able to fill Maracanã.

When I stepped onto the field and looked around the stadium, my heart beat stronger. Banners of the Universal Church from different places were spread all over the stadium. Assistants and pastors were scattered among the huge throng of people.

No space was empty. I walked slowly towards the stage; my face shone.

Recalling this scene today, I feel an unspeakable inner satisfaction. Not pride in filling the largest stadium in the world, but because God had used me. This was all I wanted, to be used by the Spirit of God to spread salvation in a world full of pain and anguish.

The people were waiting for the showdown. It began right away:

"God placed us in this world and gave us spiritual authority. The same authority given to the Lord Jesus. He did not tell His disciples to pray for the sick or demon-possessed, but ordered them to heal the sick and cast out demons."

The same deceiving spirits that were put to shame in the chains of deliverance of the Universal Church fell to their knees by the hundreds. In every part of Maracanã, men and women, teens, adults and the elderly manifested evil spirits.

Cries of joy and applause of the multitude mixed with the

voices of those who ran to a stage placed next to the stands to give testimonies about their miraculous experiences.

Afterwards, it was the time to give thanks to God.

"In a big event like this, especially in Maracanã, you normally hear, 'This is doctor so-and-so, president of this or that,' or 'This is the most honorable so-and-so,' but not here! We are all gathered here in the name of Jesus, because doctor so-and-so or this or that person cannot help you, me, or anyone. But the Lord Jesus can and will do that this morning."

The rapid applause echoed through the stadium.

"Forget about what you've done up until nine o'clock this morning. From now on, you have a chance to begin a new life. God wants to do this in you right now. God wants your life. Don't think that God is far away up in heaven, far from your pain, misery and curses. He is here right now," I continued before a silent crowd.

I ended my preaching with an injection of faith and more importantly a seed of salvation.

"It doesn't matter what religion you are, end it, whatever it is, end it. Evangelical, Catholic, spiritist, it doesn't matter. Squash it and be free. What good is it for you to clap your hands and leave here with the same life? No, this is not a show. Say, 'Jesus, I want You now.'"

The huge event was just the beginning. Eight months later, we decided to reach even higher. We announced another big meeting, this time simultaneously in Maracanã and in Maracanãzinho.

THE DESCENT

I was aware that our chains of healing and deliverance, restoration of the family and financial prosperity caused people to flock to the church, but they would only become strong after a genuine conversion. The new followers needed the Spirit of God to do battle against themselves, and to turn this new path of surrender into a permanent way of life.

Two days after Christmas 1987, we organized the largest gathering of people up to that point. We had the inspiration to pack Maracanã Stadium and Maracanãzinho at the same time with an impressive aim: to cry out for the descent of the Holy Spirit.

The invitation brought results. Over 250 thousand people turned the two major sports arenas in Rio de Janeiro into a huge sanctuary of the Universal Church.

Convoys from all over Brazil braved the intense heat of the Rio summer. As people waited for the huge meeting to start, the three electronic scoreboards of Maracanã announced what lay ahead. I asked them to write the following message:

"In a little while, the Holy Spirit will descend."

The display expressed what thousands of people were looking forward to.

"I was one of them. We left our neighborhood at three in the morning so we could find seats. When the official announcer of the stadium, the same one who announced soccer matches, read the message, it was powerful. It gave me goosebumps," Bishop Sérgio Corrêa remembers with a chuckle. He currently oversees the assistants in Brazil and the work of rescuing members who have drifted away.

I led the worship in Maracanã and Renato Maduro did it in Maracanãzinho. Our main goal was to lead a multitude of men and women to this heavenly blessing.

"The Spirit of God is at your disposal today, now. He is ready to make you a new creature. He wants to live inside of you. They may kill your body, but they can never touch your spirit. This will become your greatest treasure."

My words were followed by an unforgettable seeking of the greatest of all miracles. There were intense moments of intimacy. I wonder how many people were born of the Holy Spirit on that 27th of December.

A day to be remembered.

The sandy beaches of Rio de Janeiro also turned into settings for large events. One memorable event had a unique feature: it had no sound system. That's right. We organized a prayer vigil on Copacabana beach for more than 600,000 people, but a few hours before it began, the local residents association obtained a court order with a noise ban on our meeting.

The event was broadcast by Radio Copacabana. The members and assistants gathered in groups around large and small battery operated radios to hear my words from the stage on the sand. For anyone walking on the boardwalk, it was a strange sight—a mass of people, for the majority of the time in absolute silence, looking straight ahead.

At dawn, the crowd was still on the beach.

Those silent early morning hours caused a deafening sound in hell.

This was followed by dozens of large outdoor meetings over a period of several years—impressing religious experts, government authorities, and the press—which triggered never imagined persecutions of the Universal Church, as we will discover further ahead.

We broke attendance records at other stadiums, tens of times over in Morumbi and Pacaembu in São Paulo, the Fonte Nova in Salvador, the Mineirão in Belo Horizonte; as well as the Pinheirão in Curitiba, and the Mané Garrincha in the Federal District. The amount of people could only be compared to soccer games between the biggest rivals.

From the very beginning, we moved into a phase of over-whelming growth in Brazil.

Our march forward was rapid. In eight years there were 195 churches in 14 states of Brazil and the Federal District (capital). On average, 24 churches a year were opened, two per month, one every 15 days. In the late 1980s, the number of churches grew 2,500%.

In less than three decades, to everyone's surprise, the Universal Church became the most successful movement of faith in the country. No other evangelical church had grown so much in such a short period of time.

We adopted a slogan that became famous at that time: "The Universal Church of the Kingdom of God, where a miracle is waiting for you."

Pornographic cinemas turned into churches. Spiritist centers turned into churches. Catholic churches were turned into Universal Churches. Other evangelical churches were turned into Universal Churches. Nightclubs turned into churches. Theaters and halls all over Brazil turned into places of prayer.

In a few years, as the 1990s began, we reached more than 4,000 churches from north to south. In each city, rich or poor, urban or rural, there was a Universal Church. Currently there are over 10,000 churches nationwide in Brazil.

We focused on the project of winning the lost, on deliverance, with 24-hour television and radio programs. As I and my colleagues dedicated ourselves to the work, the Universal Church exploded—all through the guidance of the Spirit of God.

Presently, there is no stadium in the world capable of hosting one of our mega-events. In April 2004, we had one of the largest attendances: 1.5 million people filled Aterro Flamengo. In April 2010, what we referred to as "D-Day" hit new levels never reached before: 2 million people in Botafogo Bay, Rio, and 2 million in the Interlagos Circuit in São Paulo. In total, more than 8 million attended simultaneous mega-meetings throughout Brazil.

We completed a 36-year journey of unthinkable mile-stones, by the grace of our God. The phrase on the Ma-racanã Stadium scoreboards became a fact in millions of people's lives.

The Holy Spirit descended on the most distant parts of the world.

UNANSWERED TEARS

With so much growth, we faced obstacles that were hard to understand, and went through memorable experiences guided by the light of our faith.

It was Saturday, September 6, 1998, at three in the morning. I was exhausted and had just arrived at the former site of the Church in Juquitiba, São Paulo, after a week full of meetings.

"Bishop, it's awful! The roof of our church in Osasco collapsed. Nobody knows what happened," an anxious Bishop Clodomir Santos told me, taking a break from his live TV program called, "Talk and I'll Listen", to communicate this urgent information.

"Oh dear God, what happened? Is anyone injured? How are the people?"

Clodomir was stunned:

"No one knows for sure. Firefighters are attempting to rescue the wounded. People are still in the rubble. The church was packed."

I arrived in Osasco less than an hour later. The scene was devastating. Bodies were being removed from the debris... sirens and the flashing light of the firefighters, people covered in blood were being helped by the rescuers, family members in tears.

I got out of the car, took a look around and collapsed. I took off my glasses and cried. Tears were streaming down my face. I only had the strength to ask:

"Why? Why, God?"

Why were there so many deaths? Where was God's protection? The victims were praying, making their own vigil, seeking the presence of God.

The situation was mind-boggling.

The collapse of the former headquarters church in downtown Osasco left 24 people dead and over 467 injured. Over 1,400 people had been at the meeting when almost a third of the roof collapsed at around 1:45am. The roof had been held up by a wooden structure, which caused countless injuries when it fell on the people in the auditorium.

At the moment of the collapse, at the rear of the church, there arose a loud cry from the people. Everyone had just heard a message about the necessity of repentance for eternal salvation. In a short period of time, 40 vehicles and more than 180 men from the Fire Department of Osasco and of the capital city arrived on scene.

Many assistants and participants in the vigil remained to help victims get to the Emergency Room. Others rushed to the Osasco Blood Center to donate their blood. The cooperation was incredible, and the hospital soon had to turn away blood donors because the volume was so great. Donors were referred to the blood banks in nearby São Paulo.

The church had been functioning well within the building codes and guidelines. The business license issued by the local municipality was proof that there were no previous issues with the building. Then investigators presented new evidence.

"We found that the composition of the soil and nearby construction projects caused the collapse. There is no indication of negligence," said our lawyer Arthur Lavigne.

All our churches had been subjected to rigorous maintenance, and it was no different with that building, which had been rented by the church for six years. I immediately gave orders for the church to offer assistance to the victims and their families, and made sure to attend the collective funeral service in the city gymnasium.

The very morning of the catastrophe, I started talking to the families that had lost loved ones. We visited the hospitals where the injured had been taken, and emergency rooms. We prayed with every mother, father and child of the people who had been there.

We mourned with each one of them. Their pain had become my pain.

I was devastated when I arrived home that morning, not understanding the reason for so much chaos. A few hours, later I participated in a live program on TV Record and, in tears, made a pronouncement:

"Our hearts are broken. We deeply regret this accident. It's as if our own family members had died. We have visited the scene and know the pain and agony of the people. What happened was inevitable. We do not know why it happened."

"I do not know how or why it happened. I only know one thing: it was not God's punishment, because He's not a monster. He allowed this, and I don't know why."

"The people were in the middle of a prayer vigil. It's hard to understand or reason through. I don't have an answer," I ended, closing the program with a prayer for the city of Osasco.

From that day on, a turnaround occurred in the story of the Universal Church. I ordered the cancellation of leases of old buildings that did not have a rigorous structural assessment. We began dozens of construction projects throughout Brazil and around the world. We built a series of huge churches, providing comfort and above all safety, by means of the church's own department of engineering.

In Brazil alone, we have built 83 large churches in different regions of the country. Almost always, they are among the most beautiful and magnificent buildings in the city.

Even today, 15 years after that terrible accident, I do not see the logic of what happened. I cannot explain the spiritual reasons behind such a painful tragedy. But this does not in any way diminish my belief in God or my absolute trust in His Word.

Many men and women, assistants or members, carry the scars of those moments of horror on their bodies and in their minds. Even after the excruciating loss of family and friends, most remained faithful to the God we serve, without ever understanding the reason for so much pain.

Many will carry these questions to their deathbeds, but that in no way weakens the conviction of their faith. An army of warriors. An example of faithfulness and perseverance.

They, like me, repeat the conviction of the apostle Paul. What I stated the day after I saw so much suffering in the early hours of one Osasco morning is still a strong conviction within me: "All things work together for good to those who love God" (Romans 8:28).

STARS IN THE DESERT

One of the most spectacular views of the sky, dotted with stars, occurred at the top of Mount Sinai, in the Egyptian desert. Three days on only bread and water, in the company of other bishops and some Bedouin inhabitants of the arid region between Asia and Africa.

The experience was unforgettable. We meditated on the infinite sky from the same vantage point as Abraham. We had the privilege of seeing the light from the stars, such was the brightness of the sky in that utterly isolated spot. A cloud of stars with its own light. Some bigger than others, but all with a glow that brightened that desert mountain. We meditated on the Word of God. We meditated on the character of Abraham and his model of faithfulness. Ever since I surrendered to the Gospel, he has been the great reference point of the Bible for me.

We made a round-the-clock schedule so that our promise to pray every hour on the hour would be fulfilled. Every 60 minutes, a bishop or his wife would cry out for those who had made their sacrifice in our campaign of faith. We made a fire to burn the requests of the people, of which a huge volume had been brought from Brazil.

The climb was grueling. More than four hours on steep ground lined with stones. In one section of the climb, I stumbled and scraped my leg, which started bleeding immediately. But we didn't give up until we reached the summit. The temperature was another obstacle. During the day, blistering heat—at night, cold that would make your teeth chatter. The wind chill made the night even colder. The damp ground of the mountain prevented long stretches of sleep.

The food was prepared by the Bedouin: freshly baked bread on the rock surface of the mountain. Long, dirty fingernails were an insignificant detail. Ester went for almost two days without eating a thing. She ate a piece of bread only after I soaked it in olive oil. Our bathroom was behind a rock.

The same goal that drove us to climb Mount Sinai, annually leads us to various holy places of Israel, to cry out to God for the people, for the Universal Church, and for me. This journey began in December 1979 when I placed my feet in the Holy Land for the first time. The experience was amazing. Ex-bishop Rodrigues and I found an Arab taxi driver that would sell us large quantities of olive oil at a low price.

We decided to make use of this and use one of the most common symbols of faith in Brazil: olive oil. We bought 40 liters of oil in two large containers. As we were about to leave, we were stopped at the airport for a thorough check. The officials wanted to know where the oil had come from. It was a tough interrogation, with questions coming from every direction, which ended just in time for us to get on the plane. The olive oil was released moments before we boarded.

Over the years, I have returned to Israel innumerable times, but always as if for the first time. At each place we visit, I sense God Himself revealing something special deep inside of me. Mount Moriah, the Wailing Wall, Gideon's Spring, the Mount of Olives, the Jordan River, the Upper Room, the empty tomb. Our trip on April 14, 2013, brought about a completely new experience.

We climbed the highest mountain in Israeli territory: Mount Hermon. It shares a border with Lebanon and Syria and is considered to be a strategic spot for the army: the eyes of Israel. In the Bible, it is described as the site of the transfiguration, the consecration of the Lord Jesus. Hermon is clearly mentioned by the psalmist David: "Behold, how good and how pleasant it is for brethren to dwell together in unity! It is like the precious oil upon the head, running down on the beard, the beard of Aaron, running down on the edge of his garments. It is like the dew of Hermon, descending upon the mountains of Zion; for there the LORD commanded the blessing—life forevermore" (Psalm 133:1-3).

On Sunday morning we made a live broadcast, at various times of the day, for the Universal Church around the world. Standing in front of the valley and millions of viewers, I made a challenge:

"If I'm a deceiver and a thief, as people try to portray me, then nothing will happen. But if I am a servant of the Most High God, the Holy Spirit will descend on you at this moment. Your life will never be the same. I make this challenge."

I stretched out my hands from the top of Hermon. Small birds started to fly around the hill, right above us. It's a rare thing for this bird species to fly at that altitude. In churches there was a fearful silence. No music. This was not a time for emotion. An intense moment of prayer continued unbroken.

Hours later, on that same day, thousands of people reported their personal experiences with the Spirit of God on my blog. Others shared the miracle with their friends and family.

Before ending our talk, we united in a prayer for Israel.

It's a fact that mountain climbs have marked our history. In Scotland, the climb of Mount Ben Nevis, the highest in the UK, was one of the most terrifying experiences of my life. The only reason for doing it was to try and keep the doors of an important church in London open, in the neighborhood of Peckham. After ten years at the same address, the church could only continue if we bought the building. The challenge, a common procedure in England, was meant to help raise funds for the purchase of the property.

In November 2007, more than 50 people, including Cristiane my daughter and sons-in-law Renato and Julio Freitas, left on the perilous climb. We climbed at the coldest time of the year. The trip seemed impossible: rain and snow on a path full of hazards. The ground was slippery because of the large amount of ice. The physical wear and tear was tripled. At one point, Cristiane was not feeling well because of severe fatigue in her legs.

"Let's go back, Cristiane. I'll go back with you," I pleaded, with an icy wind battering our faces.

"No, Dad. I promised I would climb. I promised," she replied.

"But you are not feeling well. Let's go down," I insisted.

I had already decided to turn back. The blizzard worsened. I wore two pairs of gloves and yet it still wasn't enough to protect my hands from the cold. The danger was real: on average, five climbers a year die trying to climb Ben Nevis.

We did not turn back. The climb took over six hours. At the summit, the temperature was nine degrees below zero. Renato even made a wedding there.

"Amen, amen. You're blessed," I said, interrupting the wedding prayer, eager to begin the descent.

That was when I experienced a traumatic shock. I was walking in front of the group, with no guide, with two assistants following in my steps. All of a sudden, from one minute to the next, I felt an uncontrollable weakness. Little by little the weakness was worsening. Then I blacked out.

In the fall, I hit my head on a rock. My legs seemed to have disappeared. I came face-to-face with death. My unconsciousness lasted seconds. I had a hypoglycemic crisis that robbed me of my strength. Quickly, one of the assistants ran up to me, and by divine intervention, bit off a piece of chocolate and placed it in my mouth. I was minutes away from dying, but I didn't. I continued with the climb right through to the end.

The result is always the same: with every climb, we advance in our path of accomplishments together with those who fight with us. We do not consider any sacrifice too much in our effort to bless people. It is our pleasure. Our reward. Our salary.

Another risk I confronted was in one of the first climbs up Mount Sinai. The sun was at its peak when the camel I was riding changed direction in an instant. Camels can only climb part of the way. In an automatic reflex, one of the bishops grabbed me by the shirt and kept me from falling into the gorge below. There were over five hours of hard climbing after that fright.

I remember that day as if it were today. I carried stacks of papers containing 32 criminal accusations against me and the Universal Church. We compiled a list of the names of all who were attacking us with unfounded accusations. I climbed up Sinai in tears. There we cried out in pain and revolt against those false accusations.

On top of the mountain, together with my colleagues, I lifted up those court cases to heaven and cried out for freedom. We asked for justice. We had to make decisions about serious situations, and God honored us.

One by one, little by little, every court case and investigations was defeated. According to the Brazilian Judicial System, I was found innocent of the majority of these charges, and others were dropped for lack of evidence.

The answer came from the Holy Mountain.

To understand the suffering that we carried to the top of Sinai, that forced us to insist on an answer urgently from God, we need to go back in time.

Prepare to hear things that are hard to believe.

CHAPTER 3

THE CHALLENGE TO SURVIVE

"You planned evil against me; God planned it for good to bring about the present result—the survival of many people."

(Genesis 50:20—HCSB)

FREEDOM ON PAPER

The extraordinary growth of the Universal Church amassed an endless line of men and women that were grateful for our outreach and the mercy of God, but enemies also lined up on various fronts.

Our growth disturbed traditional religious groups that had been accustomed to their positions of influence and the slave mentality of the people, and the purchase of Record shocked the media barons—untouchable and all-powerful—who were accustomed to ruling in various spheres of influence.

The prediction was accurate: the monopoly of religion and communication was in jeopardy. We were looking forward. Brazil needed a transformation.

However there would be a price. For the Church and Record—I became target number one.

During this time, I was forced to continually have on my person an anti-arrest warrant document from the Department of Justice. My crime? Preaching the Gospel.

I have saved this document as proof of the humiliation and suffering I went through:

COURT ORDER
São Paulo
ARREST WARRANT COUNTERMAND

Case number 817/92

Police Investigation 720/92—District 27 Police

IT IS ORDERED by the official signature below, that all Officials of the Justice Department of this Court, police officers and their agents, and anyone else to whom this document is presented, that the following person be exempt from arrest: **EDIR MACEDO BEZERRA**, *son of Henrique Francisco Bezerra and Eugenia Macedo Bezerra, born in Rio de Janeiro/RJ on 02/18/45, married, religious pastor, against whom an arrest warrant was issued. In light of the Fifth Criminal Court of the Department of Justice, on 02/25/93, granting an order of Habeas Corpus number 140.760-3/0, to revoke the defendant's probation, this has been determined and issued at the present time.*

I swear this to be true under penalty of law.
February 26, 1993.

Lidia Marin Conceição Eirsinger
Judge

My freedom was contingent on a piece of paper.

Each time I wanted to leave Brazil and continue my work of spreading the gospel in other countries, I had to request permission from a judge. I was blocked from helping thousands of people around the world, teaching the Word of God, and helping social outcasts—normally the responsibility of government officials—because my freedom was partially removed. Despite my indignation at this oppression, I carefully submitted to the restrictions placed on me.

In some cases, there was police abuse. Like the night that a group of armed policemen interrupted our worship service in the Brás church, on Celso Garcia Avenue, in São Paulo, and pointed machine guns and pistols at members and assistants of the church. One of the leaders of this group took the microphone from the pastor and patted him down in rough manner. They broke into the church office, forced open the cabinets and confiscated files and computers. Ex-bishop Carlos Rodrigues was taken in handcuffs to be questioned at the police station.

What about freedom of worship and the respect for church property guaranteed by the Brazilian Constitution? No reply.

Nothing was found. This was maddening.

One day at the Tom Jobim Airport, in Rio de Janeiro, my family and I were preparing to fly to the United States, and were already seated in the plane, when federal police announced over the intercom that I had to leave the aircraft. They wanted to see my anti-arrest warrant document, with my approval to leave the country.

In a stern manner, they held back the flight for more than 30 minutes causing embarrassment and uneasiness between us, the crew, and the other passengers. It seemed premeditated, as did a flight attendant spilling coffee on my lap during one of our flights. Ester and I noticed purposeful mistreatment.

The cases relating to my alleged crimes stacked up to enormous proportions. Any accusation or comment in a newspaper would trigger a fresh investigation that forced me to constantly submit to questioning.

"Media outlets arranged for reporters to track Bishop's every step. Whenever he boarded or disembarked from a plane, reporters were there. Many times I drove him to hearings or court appearances. The pressure was far from normal," recounts Marcus Vinicius Vieira, responsible for the Universal Church in Rio for a lengthy period of time.

The vast majority of summonses were signed by the same judge: João Carlos da Rocha Mattos.

COURT ORDER
Federal Court

CONCLUSION
... *EDIR MACEDO de BEZERRA or EDIR MACEDO BEZERRA, involved in this police investigation, must present himself today at the 4th Criminal Court, in order to sign an undertaking to comply with this investigation and possible prosecution, under penalty of law.*

São Paulo, October 15, 1991.

João Carlos da Rocha Mattos
Federal Judge of the Fourth Criminal Court

The series of persecutions did not stop the Church from growing in strength, much to the contrary. On October 12, 1991, we organized a gigantic meeting at Maracanã Stadium in Rio de Janeiro, the same day that an outdoor mass was being held by the Pope in a visit to Natal, capital of the state of Rio Grande do Norte.

Our event had been confirmed for a number of months, though various government officials had tried to pressure us into canceling it. I received constant phone calls from powerful men in Brasília predicting that the Maracanã meeting would end up provoking the Vatican. I did not care. The aim was to glorify the Lord Jesus.

After arriving from the United States, where I preached in a small church in New York City, my attorneys informed me that I had to testify in yet another hearing. This was three days before our event. All of a sudden, the Federal Police delayed the questioning.

The night before the Maracanã meeting, as I was inviting listeners of Radio Copacabana to the event, I was informed about an unexpected and unthinkable arrest warrant. I had been charged for failing to appear for questioning. It was hard to believe, but the police were searching for me at that moment. I was told to voluntarily turn myself in to the authorities to avoid an arrest that would cause a firestorm.

Immediately, Ester and I went undercover. I spent the night hiding in Niterói. On the day of the event, I was unable to get anywhere near Maracanã. Hours before the meeting, one of the pastors called to tell me that he had seen federal agents spread around the stadium, waiting to ambush me.

"The idea seemed to be to make the arrest inside Maracanã, which would have led to so much confusion. It was the most aggressive way to damage the image of Bishop and the

Church," recalls Bishop Honorilton Gonçalves, who followed these events closely.

My absence did not prevent a magnificent meeting for the glory of the Holy Spirit. The stands were filled with over 150 thousand people while in Natal, the Pope gathered less than 90 thousand. This comparison was noted in the Brazilian and even international press.

I spent the weekend in hiding and changed my address three different times. Whenever we were in the car and passed someone that looked suspicious, I would have to hide my face. At gas stations, I was forced to hide like a criminal. I lived this way for three days. Many cannot imagine the amount of humiliation Ester and I have lived through.

Early Sunday morning I traveled by car to São Paulo to present myself at the headquarters of the Federal Police in the center of town. The day was filled with depositions. That Monday, I arrived home exhausted and told Ester I had had enough of running from the police. We spoke about the justice of God and how we were suffering for a great cause that we had embraced on behalf of the less fortunate.

We decided to pour out our hearts to our Lord.

That night, soon after praying, the phone rang:

"Sir, I need you to return to the station right away. The judge is threatening to revoke your release permit, and is saying he might even issue another arrest warrant," said one of the lawyers.

Hours after leaving the Federal Police, I was forced to return.

I arrived back home in the early hours of the morning. My face was expressionless. I felt like a nobody, worse than the filth of the sewer. I confess that my strength was about to give out.

I cried before God.

I asked why there had been so much bitterness and shame.

While riding the elevator of the Radio Copacabana building in Rio de Janeiro, I wished I could be the elevator operator. "He has more reason to be happy than me. My God, I want to be like this man!" I thought. The size of this torment awakened a base aspect of myself. At times I wished I could be a stray dog wandering about the street.

Honestly, if I had not believed in God, I would have put a bullet in my head or had a heart attack. Suicidal thoughts drifted through my mind.

I remembered my encounter with God. Only the Lord Jesus could give me the strength I needed, would renew me so that I could face all this pain. The Word of God would not fail. What I had pursued was a single goal: to bring salvation to the lost, and to offer a real faith that had the power to transform lives inside and out.

The Holy Spirit could not turn His back on my goals.

My prayer—published in the *Folha Universal*, second edition, March 1992—was an expression of the torture I felt. The title said it all: "The Supplication of a Troubled Soul".

"O Lord, my God and my Father, in this time of sadness and pain, my soul comes to You.

It's a fact, Lord, that there is nothing good in me, nothing praiseworthy to present to You. In the light of Your presence all my good deeds are an embarrassment.

Lord, turn You ear to my cry for the sake of Your beloved Son, Jesus Christ! How can those who go to the grave glorify Your name? How can those in darkness reveal Your wonders?

And yet Lord, I accept Your invitation that says, "Call upon Me in the day of trouble; I will deliver you, and you shall glorify Me,' and so I make this appeal: help me Lord, once again, for my soul is lost.

Extend Your forgiveness to me and save me from the relentless persecution of my enemies, who are stronger than me.

Oh Lord, when I arise from this awful tribulation, I intend to do nothing more than to glorify You forever.

I thank You in advance for all that You are going to do, in the name of the Lord Jesus Christ.

Amen, Bishop Macedo"

One month later, on April 19 of the same year, I published another prayer. It was a request for divine intervention.

"O Lord, my God and my Father, for the love of Your name, save me! I am at death's door.

I am like a leaf that's blown by the wind, scorched by the heat of the sun—I feel trampled by the thugs of this world, broken into pieces.

I am hit again and again by powerful blasts of wind, and scattered in shreds…

This is my life, a life of turmoil; problems come from every direction.

Lord, whenever I start to think that death would be a welcome reward, someone reminds me of Your name and… once again hope dawns.

Stretch out Your hand to me, Lord, and repair the broken pieces of my life.

May the dew of heaven fall on me, create new life in me, and graft me back into the true vine.

I have no one else to call out to… if You disappoint me… I will disappear forever.

Bishop Macedo"

God repaired my broken pieces. He did not disappoint me.

The charges against me were of every kind and from every direction. Some were the very height of absurdity and discrimination.

In the document that authorized placing me behind bars, the sheer number of controversial claims must have broken some record. A substitute judge of only 31 years of age, who was in office for only one month, signed the document. My prison stay, as has already been explained in Nothing to Lose 1, occurred in May of 1992.

Below I have highlighted some of the arguments that the judge used to support his request for my arrest:

COURT ORDER
São Paulo

**The Twenty-first Criminal Court of the Central Capital
Case number 298/92**

Defendant: Edir Macedo Bezerra

The summary of the decision and arguments can be found below:

...]... in the body of the accusation, we have technical data that points to the manner in which the spirits of inept people are influenced, leading to an astounding growth of the flock of followers...]... which leads to even more damage, since these people do not have the adequate or necessary sociocultural base to deliver them from evil...]... Under an amalgamation of religious denominations, in essence, the referred to institution misleads its respective followers, proclaiming miracles, impossible healings, in short, an unbelievable series of occurrences for the institution's own interests...

...]... Unfortunately the numerous, shocking actions of the denomination appeal to the varied interests of an uncountable number of people...]...

... Social class breakdown, rapidly increasing inflation and recession, lead to the uncontrollable spread of legions, which under the guise of announcing the good news, preach concepts that lead to control, and actual brain-washing...]... in light of these arguments and the analysis of the attached evidence, and the additional revelations, I order the arrest of the defendant.

São Paulo, May 22, 1992.

Carlos Henrique Abrão
Judge

I respect all members of the judiciary and trust in the sovereignty and competence of the Brazilian justice system, but I have the right to expose what I consider pure discrimination that led to those days of distress behind bars.

I would need thousands of pages to recount the real and impressive testimonials of the men and women who have been transformed by the power of faith that have been taught in meetings of the Universal Church. Ask these people if they would trade the lives they have today with those of their past. Ask them if they're happier today, or when they didn't have the belief that they gained from us.

It's a simple question of logic. If I deceive and exploit the many destroyed people who come, why do they stay in the church? If people were deceived once by me, they would never come back again. Why then, are so many of our churches packed out in Brazil? Why are there so many members of the church who have been faithful for decades? Why are there many doctors, dentists, lawyers, teachers, advertising executives, entrepreneurs, academics and other intellectuals among us? How can our growth throughout the world among different cultures races and languages be explained?

This is not the fulfillment of a promise of Bishop Macedo in their lives; it's the fulfillment of the Word of God.

How can we not think of the apostles and the Lord Jesus Himself, who had been arrested for spreading life-changing faith?

Aside from how our convictions may appear, take an impartial look at the social work of the church that reaches all areas of society. How many billions does the government save because of the spiritual help given by the Universal Church? Has anyone thought of this? When someone overcomes chronic depression, or a drug addiction, how much does the health care system save? What is the cost of rehabilitating an inmate or a juvenile delinquent through a broken prison system?

Imagine this effect multiplied by millions. Is it hard to picture?

The Universal Church bases its beliefs on the teachings of the Word of God 100%. In the Bible itself, there are clear and incontestable examples of faith that brought about healings and deliverance. Today we have irrefutable accounts of people who have experienced miracles and who can attest to the veracity of these promises.

Did the Lord Jesus brainwash people?

The Universal Church is a spiritual emergency room. It was birthed by a sincere desire to help those who felt lost. This is what first happened to me when I was still young, when I was a government employee. I was inwardly transformed through my experience with the God of the Bible.

I decided to do the Work of God solely out of a desire to convey a message that was intelligent, that could transform lives. This is the greatest miracle: to gain a new life, a complete transformation of thoughts and values, able to cause a radical turnaround in the way we live, an inner state of happiness and understanding that only the Spirit of God can produce in a person. Only those who have experienced this gift know what I'm talking about.

How many of those who frequent the church are found drunk behind the wheel, threatening the lives of innocent people? How many commit crimes and tragedies because of drug addictions? How many commit armed atrocities against society? How many have appeared in daily police blotters? What religion do these types of people belong to?

The Universal Church of the Kingdom of God is the work of the Spirit of God, not of man. Not of Bishop Macedo.

A NEW ERA

I'm attracted to weather's ferocity. In spite of the danger, lightning storms are spectacular. At times, I watch the force of lightning striking the earth from my window at home. Lightning is nothing more than a high intensity electrical charge traveling across the atmosphere. Most lightning bolts just strike between clouds. Few actually strike the ground. But when these sparks from heaven hit the earth, they can cause great destruction.

Faith is like lightning. When awakened, it acts quickly and strikes at evil with immeasurable force. It is impossible to contain lightning, just as it is impossible to contain those who live by faith.

The purchase of Record Network was like lightning, and produced a wave of attacks, from various enemies. After the station was paid for—by means of God's response, described in the beginning of this book—I faced another barrage when we tried to transfer the concession to my name. A concession is the permission to operate television channels within the country, and is controlled by the government.

The newspaper *O Estado de S. Paulo*, on March 29, 1992, published an article entitled, "Who Wants It," by journalist Nirlando Beirão, that conveyed the shadowy interests of those days:

"It will not be easy for Bishop Macedo to renew TV Record's concession, which ends this year. Not only because of the fusillade of attacks against him and his Universal Church of the Kingdom of God, but because of so many envious, influential people. In addition to the insistent José Carlos Martinez, of Grupo OM do Paraná—who is temporarily, but only temporarily requesting a ride for TV Gazeta in São Paulo—a handful of businessmen have gathered around the president's brother, Leopoldo Collor de Mello, who are interested in the television spoils of the bishop."

The news revealed the size of my obstacle to obtain the concession. We had stringently adhered to the law, there was nothing out of line, but we had to wait for the approval of President Fernando Collor. The document was stuck at the Secretary of Communication's offices, what is now known as the Ministry of Communication. The Secretary at that time had publicly revealed that there was opposition to the transfer to my name. According to him, he was being secretly pressured by major media groups and businessmen, who had designs for the television market.

Everyone was just waiting for any kind of misstep on my part. But the Holy Spirit was my guide.

One of them was the businessman, José Carlos Martinez, owner of CNT, National Television Center, and one of the campaign treasurers of Fernando Collor. Martinez wanted to turn his TV station in Paraná into a large national network. But for that to happen, he needed a powerful station in São Paulo. Of course that would be Record.

One day, he called an emergency meeting with me in the former headquarters of TV Miruna in the São Paulo neighborhood of Moema.

Martinez stated explicitly that the government would not sign the concession for Record.

I politely listened to the businessman for a few minutes.

"I can't help you, sir. There's no way the government will sign this, you can be sure of that. I have my sources. You don't have the least chance, Bishop," he confirmed, excited about his prospects.

All of a sudden, I interrupted his tiresome string of defeatist words, stood up from my place on the sofa and said:

"Listen closely Martinez, the only way Record will not be mine is over Jesus' dead body!"

The man left the meeting irritated.

Similar discussions took place with officials of Record who had inherited the station from the former administration. In front of a crowd of TV journalists, I explained my intention of making a large investment in the company. As I was speaking, two or three professionals poked fun at me as they puffed on cigarettes with feet on the chairs, blowing smoke into the air. During the conversation, one of them asked me:

"How can you be so sure Record will be placed in your name? We'd all like to know. What guarantee do you have that the government will give you this concession? What guarantee do we have?"

I became impatient.

"Only if God is not God!"

During this wait for the concession, a suspicious fire broke out in the Record building in August 1992. Part of the Record Theater along Miruna Avenue was affected. There were no victims of the fire, and within a few hours, firefighters had it under control. The press reported that the fire was a result of arson, and accused us as the ones who had set it to receive insurance money. Quickly, a new charge was made against me. I was suspect number one of the crime. Two facts knocked down these accusations. The first was that I was in New York City during the fire, and the second, which was irrefutable, was that we were late in the payments of that particular part of our insurance policy. Why would I set fire to a property that was not covered by insurance?

One more attack to create a scandal, and who knows, to snatch Record away from me.

Within a week, the Federal Police and the Treasury Police of São Paulo arrived and jointly asked for the documents of the concession process. Demerval Gonçalves remembers that he was called to Brasília in a mysterious signaling of PC Farias:

"He explicitly stated that the concession would have a price. It was an obvious request, and of course we didn't give a single penny to the treasurer. We don't work this way."

Everyone wanted to take advantage of our situation. President Collor had promised support, even after breaking some promises. Before the election of 1989, I had believed in the project of the governor. Our first official conversation occurred in Rio de Janeiro.

"We're going to help you, Collor, but I want to ask you something," I told him.

"Of course Bishop, I'm at your disposal," responded the then candidate.

"I want to make a prayer on the day of your inauguration as president. It will be the first time that a pastor prays for a leader of our nation right after he walks up the ramp at Palácio do Planalto," I explained, imagining how many lives could be reached with that act of evangelism.

"Consider it done. I agree, it's done," assured Collor reaching out his hand to seal the agreement.

I returned the gesture. In the following months, I personally promoted the Collor campaign. I made public my vote for him. I was even photographed embracing the candidate, wearing a campaign t-shirt, with the traditional slogans in green and yellow.

Collor won the election. On January 1, 1990, inauguration day, he ignored my request and walked up the ramp, accompanied on the left by former witch, Maria Cecília Silva, "Mother Cecília", famous for rituals that "helped" politicians and other personalities to rise to power. In a recent interview with the media, his ex-wife, Rosane Collor, even stated that the gardens of Casa da Dinda (the Collor family mansion) were commonly used for grotesque rituals of black magic and animals sacrificed to spirits.

Three years later, I needed Collor to sign the concession. I was sure that God would not abandon us, even when we were in the eye of a storm of accusations.

In May of 1992, the month that I had been imprisoned, a wave of serious allegations were made against Pedro Collor, the president's brother, that directly involved Farias. The CPI in Congress, forced by protests in the street, moved to impeach him towards the end of that year.

Days before being removed from office, Collor invited me for morning coffee in Brasília, at the home of former Congressman Paulo Octávio. The president arrived by helicopter. He said he was outraged at the Globo Network, which from one moment to the next stopped their support of him. On that occasion, I made a strong prayer laying both my hands on the head of Collor.

In the end, he acted honorably towards me, and Record. Before leaving, I gave him this advice:

"President, do as I do. Stop 'drinking the wine' of bad news in the press. This is how we keep ourselves safe."

The signature for the concession was practically the last act of Collor as president. Our Lord is faithful.

Currently, in private conversations with businessmen, officials of the judiciary and political figures, including governors, senators, ministers and many presidents and former presidents, I hear the same comments, and sometimes

A period of suffering during the purchase of Record. The attacks came from all sides. The Bible was my refuge. "Blessed are you when they revile and persecute you, and say all kinds of evil against you falsely for My sake. Rejoice and be exceedingly glad, for great is your reward in heaven, for so they persecuted the prophets who were before you." (Matthew 5.11,12).

PODER JUDICIÁRIO
SÃO PAULO
Vigésima Primeira Vara Criminal Central da Capital

Processo nº 298/92
Autora : Justiça Pública
Réu : Edir Macedo Bezerra
Artigos: 171,"caput",combinado com 71 "caput",combinado com 29 "
caput",artigo 288,II (todas as figuras),combinado com 71
caput" e 29 "caput",todos combinados com 69,"caput",do
Código Penal Brasileiro.

Vistos,etc:
MINISTÉRIO PÚBLICO DO ESTADO DE -
SÃO PAULO,com base nos artigos epigrafados,formula denúncia criminal contra a pessoa de EDIR MACEDO BEZERRA,vulgo Bispo Macedo,
líder da Igreja Universal do Reino de Deus.Em apertada síntese -
a Justiça Pública,após relatar as atividades desempenhadas,sob o
pretexto religioso,desnuda a atividade levada a efeito pela sei-
ta,irrogando ao increpado as práticas dos delitos de estelionato,
curandeirismo e charlatanismo,suscitando o modo peculiar adstri-
to ao "modus operandi",de tal arte bastante peculiar a ponto de cau-
sar o desmesurado crescimento do seu número de adeptos;dessarte -
os subscritores da exordial aguardam,com o recebimento e proces,
mento da presente ação penal,seu encaminhamento normal até a eta
pa de ulterior condenação(fls.2/16).
A vestibular acusatória está acom-
panhada de variegados documentos e testemunhas de pessoas que, de
alguma forma,conhecem o mecanismo de funcionamento da entidade re
ligiosa,inclusive no seu bojo estão subsídios técnicos que apon-
tam,"si et in quantum", o modo de influenciar no espírito daque-
las pessoas hipossuficientes,levando com que o rebanho de fiéis -
se alastre assustadoramente.
Sobredito material foi pausada e
detidamente analisado,cotejando-se-o com os demais subsídios que,
nessa etapa preambular,irradiam dados atinentes à natureza da res
pectiva "opinio delicti".
A "persecutio criminis" encontra-
se espelhada,à saciedade,no procedimento investigatório,compondo
se os autos de quatro volumes,sendo certo que estamos no momento
oportuno para efeito de exame acurado,sob o ângulo do recebimento da denúncia e outras providências correlatas que a espécie -
está a comportar.

Unpublished documents. Accusations were always filled with prejudice. Nothing was ever proven.

PODER JUDICIÁRIO
JUSTIÇA FEDERAL

Seção Judiciária: São Paulo
4ª Vara Criminal

ALVARÁ DE SOLTURA

O(A) Doutor(a) JOÃO CARLOS DA ROCIA MAT
TOS
Juiz Federal da Vara acima referida, na forma da
lei, etc.

MANDA ao Diretor/Delegado de Polícia Federal em SP
ou quem suas vezes fizer, ao lhe ser apresentado, ponha in-
continenti em liberdade, se por outro motivo não dever permanecer preso, EDIR MACEDO
leira, natural de , estado civil , nacionalidade brasi-
são e empregador , com anos de idade, filho de , profis-
tador(a) da Cédula de Identidade - Registro Geral nº expedida pelo
19 , al recolhido(a) desde o dia de de 19 , em decorrência
tendo em vista que, por despacho proferido nos autos do Processo nº 91-0301357-2
, à disposição deste Juízo, de
ta data, revogando a prisão temporária decretada contra o seg
CUMPRA-SE, na forma e sob as penas da lei, certificando (s) o(s) interessado (s) de que este
Juízo funciona no Forum de Justiça Federal, localizado na Pça. da República nº
299 - Centro São Paulo
EXPEDIDO nesta cidade de São Paulo
, em 15 de outubro de 1991
Eu, Na. Sília B. Farias
Aux. Judiciária
eu, datilografei e conferi. E
, Bel. Valmir Luis Fere
ino , Diretor(a) de Secretaria, reconferi e subscrevo.

JOÃO CARLOS DA ROCIA MATTOS
JUIZ FEDERAL

My freedom
revolved around
a piece of paper.
I was forced
to carry an
Arrest Warrant
Countermand
to avoid being
detained on the
street.

ESSA EU NÃO SAI
A. GLOBO. USOU MI
FUNDO DE GARANT

ABAIXO GLOBO
O POVO NÃO É BOBO

In 1995, Globo used heavy artillery, even distorting facts such as the bags of requests at Maracanã. In the mini-series *Decadência*, a bra was thrown on top of the Bible. People took to the streets in our defense.

Climbs up Mount Sinai always marked my life. With every visit to this holy place, there was a new conquest. The climb is dangerous, the temperature is an obstacle, but I refused to give up even with an injured leg.

Every time we climb a mountain we have a goal. Above: on Ben Nevis in Scotland, keeping the doors of a London church open. Center: an evening on Sinai. Side: Mount Hermon, the tallest in Israel, we had a very special goal.

The arrival of the gospel to isolated tribes of Africa brought me to tears. No roof and benches made from tree trunks, the Universal Church accomplishes the same mission: saving souls.

Jesus Cristo é o Senhor
Igreja universal do Reino de Deus

In May of 2013, more than 70 thousand people packed the Pavilhão do Anhembi in São Paulo in a meeting to rescue the suffering.

The Temple of Solomon in March of 2013 with fifty percent of the work completed. Every aspect of this construction is holy.

During one of my last visits I examined every inch of the building. Solomon's Temple will be open for all people of every religion.

The first time I stepped onto the altar of the Temple of Solomon I remembered our beginning in the old funeral parlor: a man cannot do this.

even a "thank you", which brings me a sense of great achievement.

What would Brazil be in these last years without Record Network? How many restraints and excesses were avoided in the fight against Globo, a communication monopoly? Its control of information always elected and pulled down politicians. It always raised up and stepped on whoever caught its eye. Who denies this? The country finally stopped being held hostage to this monopoly and its evils.

The growth of Record transformed Brazil. It generated employment. It encouraged culture and diversity. It gave free access to information. It encouraged competition.

My declared income on my Tax Returns and on Record's taxes, filed with Internal Revenue, show that I have never taken a penny from Record as salary or profit sharing. As a shareholder I have always reinvested the profits into the station. More than 4,000 employees produce 85 hours of domestic content in Brazil. The signal coverage reaches 98% of the country and is produced by 99 stations and their affiliates. The international signal reaches 125 countries on four continents.

It is the second most-watched television station in Brazil, with respected journalists whose reports have repercussions throughout Brazil and abroad.

I was a victim of a monopoly that did everything in its power to wipe me off the map, as we will better understand in the next few pages, analyzing the events of 1995 with caution and symbolism. Even today, now and then, new defamation attacks are mounted, but they no longer have the same strength.

The same arguments, the same tricks, the same list of wrongs.

Brazil has woken up thanks to the existence of Record. Thanks to our God.

WHO WOULD PUT UP WITH THIS?

I credit much of the bad image given to the church at the
beginning of my evangelistic work to the avalanche of
negative reports in the biased Brazilian media. I have no
doubt that if the Universal Church had begun in the United
States, England or any other nation without a strong Catholic tradition, it would be much more respected today, and
maybe even admired from the very outset. Not that this is
important to me, but it is a cry for justice.

The press was biased against us, even before the purchase
of Record. Today there are remnants of that time, though on
a smaller scale—with the exception of TV Globo, that treats
us as competitors in business and ideology.

The first blatant attack on television happened on the
program "Documento Especial" ("Special Documentary",
in English), of the now bankrupt TV Machete. For more
than one hour we were labeled as fanatics and leaders of a
church of the pathetic. Our work of deliverance was indi-
rectly labeled a farce.

In June 1990, I was invited to participate in a debate program with a large audience at that time. It was hosted by

Silvia Popovic on prime time, on the SBT channel. It was agreed with the production team that I would discuss faith and religion, which I saw as an opportunity to explain the principles of belief in the gospel more clearly, to a wider audience.

I was far too naïve.

Right away, as the host announced the theme of the program, I was startled:

"Society returns together with its leaders to a controversial and frightening subject that we have put up for debate today: the growth of evangelical cults, in particular, the Universal Church of the Kingdom of God. What is happening to Brazil?" asked the host.

The surprises did not stop there. To my amazement the presenter took an accusatory stance:

"One of the criticisms made of you, sir, is that many people are tricked, extorted and forced to give their tithes to receive healing. And when they wake up to the fact, they are paying for a miracle that does not always happen. There are a series of accusations against your church. I would like to know, what have you to say to these accusations?"

The same old accusations as always. By my side stood the participants in the debate: an actress, another pastor, and two congressmen, one of them being the ex-presidential candidate Roberto Freire.

I asked the presenter to show me my accusers and argued the obvious. The proof that the work of the Universal Church is serious, its continued growth and the vast number of transformed lives.

The presenter then revealed a woman in the studio, disguised with sunglasses and a wig, who said that she had been a victim of the Church. She alleged that her daughter had been told to abstain from everything, and to cut herself off from society—a sob story.

The most irritating thing was to see the applause of the audience, obviously orchestrated by the production team to provoke me.

Then a police chief came out, the same one who had invaded our church with machine guns, with new accusations that didn't make the slightest bit of sense.

"The policeman says that we hand out flyers about the sale of holy oil and miraculous healings, but he doesn't have any proof. Where is the flyer?" I asked, interrupting the policeman various times.

The flyer, of course, never appeared. At the end of the program, the host was sought out by Plenitude Magazine for an interview, who immediately responded:

"About the Universal Church? No! I don't have patience for this now…"

This program, and many other reports of that time, showed an embarrassing side to the press and exposed its blatant religious bias.

A famous congressman then, Afanásio Jazadi, was one of the people in the media who pushed for this bias the most. He used a radio program to systematically attack us and tried to draft laws to hinder the preaching of the gospel. His program grew to one of the largest radio audiences in Brazil, and was the most voted for congressman in São Paulo, but used this to disparage our spiritual work. His statements in the press, especially on TV, were always charged with hatred and contempt. They were many. All of them were malicious, and always with the goal of labeling our pastors and myself as criminals. The sadistic pleasure and bitterness of his words caught my attention. What happened to him will be revealed in the coming pages.

The Universal Church and I were continuously slandered, and were denied the right to defend ourselves. The exceptions to this were extremely rare.

I have gathered a selection of passages from columns and editorials from the major newspapers in Brazil during the 1990s. Pay close attention to the tone of the content:

Journal do Brasil, April 24, 1991
Edir Macedo Bezerra: A nobody turns spiritual leader

Diário Popular, May 4, 1992
Scumbag preaching

O Globo, April 29, 1991
Salvation for sale at the supermarket
"...]... These miracle cures are classified by some theologians as 'perverse practices' and 'ploys of manipulation'...]... The Universal Church is a part of a group of cults that sells salvation, that thrives on the backs of the poor..."

Tithing, an investment portfolio
"...]... For the flock that follows the pastors of the Uni-

versal Church, it's rare to leave the meeting without first being sheared."

Notícias Populares, May 5, 1991
Religious ruse under police observation
"If you're desperate, buy yourself a miracle, or go to an auction for divine prosperity…"

O Estado de São Paulo,

May 21, 1989
Samba dancers now sing Hallelujah

November 11, 1989
Record becomes Kingdom of God TV

October 19, 1991
Rap sheet: Pastor Edir Macedo called in to testify

January 30, 1992
Bishop Edir Macedo stretches out his tentacles

April 23, 1992
Prosperous venture
"… The leadership of Mr. Edir Macedo would not have grown to such dimensions had there not been, in the first place, such great spiritual need, because the poorest and most ignorant strata of society go to him, who are always in search of saviors and miracle workers able to heal their ills…"

May 23, 1992
Advantageous providence
"… When it comes to the gifts of the Holy Spirit, the 'bishop' knows nothing. In compensation, he has other gifts that enable him to enjoy prosperity and affluence at the expense of the people's belief…"

June 29, 1990
The "bishop" has a psychiatric disorder
"… The head of investigations of Polinter (Brazil's interstate police) sent out a press release stating that he has asked for a psychiatric evaluation of Edir Macedo, due to what he sees as 'psychopathic, sociopathic and amoral behavior'. He is still considering bringing a charge against the leader of the Universal Church for the practice of mind control on his followers."

Note the sarcastic and disrespectful tone in which we were treated over the years. Not even corrupt politicians or cruel murderers were branded this way on the pages of these newspapers. All of this libel and slander was in reaction to a work uniquely geared to rescuing the desperate with the preaching of the gospel, and filling the social gap left by inept government leaders.

Would you have put up with this?

THE MASSACRE

F rom the time we took over Record, Globo (the rival media giant), began direct frontal attacks against me and the Universal Church. But from 1995, the attacks rose to a higher caliber. That was the exact year that Record Network became the third ranking television broadcaster in Brazil and was preparing for even more promising growth spurts.

The punches were now below the belt and direct. The founder of Globo himself confessed to the coming threat, as is revealed in this excerpt in a report published in September 1995.

"Globo tries to exhibit a sense of calm, which is only superficial. Roberto Marinho spoke confidentially to a friend, that in the next ten years, Record would become the network with the greatest armament to threaten the predominance of his station."
("Merciless War", *IstoÉ* Magazine)

The logic was best explained in the words of the reputed critic of culture and television in an article that came out on January 13, 1996.

"Record Network is the mover and shaker of the common people, and plans to become the new leader of the public. It is in a political power struggle with Globo. On Brazilian TV, the most precious currency is not Ibope (the Brazilian television ratings system), nor is it money, but political power. Record has brought to the screen those who have been excluded, those who Madame Globo TV hates to show. Christians, traditionally ignored by the educated and well dressed, have now entered the scene. And it's against this scene that Globo is moving.

("Fine Symphony", Eugenio Bucci, *O Estado do S. Paulo*)

That monopoly would not be able to hold its ground without orchestrating a severe retaliation. Is there any doubt that Globo Network only attacks me and the Universal Church because of Record?

To understand—at least somewhat—the intolerable behind-the-scenes actions of Globo Network in 1995, watch the shocking British documentary, *Beyond Citizen Kane*, which was legally banned in Brazil by the Rio-based broadcast company. Produced in 1992, the video is available on the internet and reveals the origins of entrepreneur Roberto Marinho's power. It is so revealing that every Brazilian, and those interested in the Church, should take out time to watch it.

1995 was a long year.

In the following pages, I list the five main branches of the Globo Organization, in chronological order, discussing the finer points of this wave of attacks from a viewpoint that has never been revealed before.

A version that explains the target of this bombardment—18 years after the fact—needs to be entered into the recent history of Brazil. The abuses of a media group that had absolute control over information for years, need to be spelled out and passed down to the next generations.

A lesson needs to be learned.

A PACK OF LIES

The entire year of 1995 was punctuated by reports against the Universal Church in the newscasts and programs of Globo Network. Their tactic was one of reopening old wounds—from April 1992, a month before my arrest—when the main newscast of the station aired a long report about one of our meetings in Maracanã Stadium.

The reporter highlighted, *ad nauseam*, images of various pastors carrying bags full of prayer requests. According to Globo Network, these bags were full of money. The event, according to the narrator, was a series of improper incidences, and a fanatical crowd deceived by the words of a "criminal".

In the year following the purchase of Record Network, a weekly 60-minute program treated the church as a "police investigation" and used the worst adjectives when referring to me. On the day of my arrest, they were the only news network that had a team positioned at the exact police station where I was taken. No other media outlet was there. In July 1995, producers infiltrated our churches and illegally recorded meetings with a hidden camera. The intention was to show, once again, that members were "deceived and forced to make financial contributions". They had a long report on their Sunday program.

In the following years, more large and small reports, on Globo Television and through its newspaper branch, revealed that the guns were still being pointed at me.

The hardest thing for Globo, in my opinion, must have been to see the uninterrupted growth of the Universal Church in spite of all their accusations. The stigma of prison did not shut the doors of the Church; on the contrary, it brought even further growth. Churches were overcrowded with new believers united in the fight against the unfair assaults. It was a milestone in our growth. And Record, only recently brought to life, strengthened its projects for television, which would directly affect the power of the Rio-based group (Globo).

For those who ruled the country, they were subject to the constant actions of that media giant, raising up and sacking businessmen, judges, congressmen, governors, ministers, and even presidents of the Republic—hostages to the monopoly—this could not have been an easy scene to watch.

They could only resort to organizing more ammunition.

A REAL-LIFE SOAP OPERA

This is an exact description of the scene. Nothing was removed or added.

"The pastor enters the room and starts to flirt with a woman that feels trapped.

The woman was the maid, the same woman who had helped raise him.

The pastor seduces the woman. Both passionately embrace each other.

As she removes her clothes, the woman tosses her bra on the pastor's Bible, which lays open on the bed where the couple then sleeps together for the first time.

The camera slowly pans across the bra tossed on the Bible."

A scandalous show without precedent on Brazilian television, which few remember. What did this mean?

It was an affront to the greatest symbol of the Christian faith—a slap in the face of every man and woman who cared about the sanctity of the Word of God. The Bible is not a book of life only for the Universal Church, but for all people who are faithful to the gospel all over the world.

What happened in response? Nothing!

Many applauded Globo, and even credited the station for its beautiful and creative poetic license. And yet it violated one of the most sacred symbols of Christianity. In other countries, this TV broadcaster would have been severely punished.

It was in that climate of indignation and contempt that I heard about the miniseries "Decadência" ("Decadence"), aired by Globo Network in September of 1995. The main character of the plot was a corrupt, immoral pastor, and the leader of a church of unstable people.

Undoubtedly, I was the target.

The 12-part miniseries was written by author Dias Gomes.

It was a mocking caricature of my life as an evangelical preacher. A satire of my values, and worst of all, the principles of God's Word. Several entire conversations of mine from an interview with a weekly magazine were reproduced by the main character of this miniseries:

September 9, 1995
Folha de S. Paulo
"Decadence" uses phrases of bishop
"Excerpts from an interview of Edir Macedo in 1990 have been added to the work of Dias Gomes, creator of the Globo Network miniseries, revealing to whom this production is really directed."

When the amount of unease this attack generated became evident, Globo included an audio in the opening credits of "Decadence" that was read by the actor who played the main character:
"It is essential to reassert our respect for all religions."

It seemed like an emotional appeal to the gullible.

The following years brought more mockery, insults and fictional fabrications. In the miniseries "Ó Paí, Ó!" (a Bahian slang meaning, "You must be joking!"), a con artist became a corrupt pastor who embezzled money from his church. In the soap opera "Duas Caras" ("Two Faces"), a radical, hate-filled pastor urged his followers to acts of violence, some of which were an attempted lynching and hate crimes against homosexuals. These were just a few examples. At the same time, Catholic saints and symbols were always treated with care and reverence in the plots and by characters of their television dramas.

Curiously, only now, after a long history of launching attacks, this same broadcaster has begun to sponsor major Contemporary Christian music events. Very strange, isn't it? Can the intentions of this company be trusted?

INCITEMENT

It was nighttime in the United States when I received a call from São Paulo about the firestorm from Globo Network's nightly news show. One of our former bishops had lightly tapped a three-foot high image of a saint with his foot, an image that he had purchased. It was October 12, 1995, a Catholic holy day. Basing his arguments on verses in the Bible, he had criticized the worship of saints.

There could only have been a few televisions tuned in to the Church's program on Record in the early morning hours of that day. But the facts were exaggerated to their full extent by one newscaster:

"A Bishop of the Universal Church of the Kingdom of God creates controversy and outrage across the country! He used an image of Our Lady of Aparecida to accuse the Catholic Church of profiting from the worship of saints. He used aggressive gestures to back up his arguments on camera."

The story was picked up by all the other Rio-based broadcasters and the image of him kicking the statue were endlessly repeated, without fail, over the following days. The goal was to turn Catholics against us.

Assistants and pastors were asked not to appear in public wearing uniforms that identified them as belonging to the Church. Church members were thrown out of their homes by their families. I publically admitted that it had been a mistake. I immediately apologized on television and radio, explaining that we have serious disagreements with the doctrines taught by the Vatican with respect to faith in the Word of God, but that we love Catholics just as much as we love members of Universal, and those who are lost in other religions of the world.

I also apologized on a nationwide broadcast of Record. And we did more; I told Record to offer the Catholic Church of São Paulo the same ten minutes in which this incident occurred. The offer was declined.

We tried to be open-minded and to request peace, but we were misinterpreted. I did not understand. I kept asking myself if the Vatican had forgiven Globo for showing a bra tossed on the Bible a few months prior to that, in the "Decadence" airings. But there was no need for forgiveness, after all, there had never been an outcry over the insult and abuse of one of the most sacred symbols of Christianity.

The article below was published on Sunday, November 5, 1995, and though it is somewhat abrasive, it makes some interesting comments on certain aspects of the discord sparked by the Rio broadcaster:

Folha de S. Paulo
Unquestionable miracle!
Ombudsman Marcelo Leite
"… Those clumsy kicks with the side of his shoe and those unconvincing punches gave me the same awkward feeling I get when I watch the melodrama of a Mexican soap opera.

They are not all that convincing.

The pastor was a victim of television's ability to take facts to the extreme. By exhaustive repetition, Globo has managed to transform an innocuous gesture into a crime against God.

What we should not lose sight of amid the great amount of drivel and venom from Cid Moreira, is that the first stone came from Globo, sugar-coated, disguised and veiled in the miniseries "Decadence".

The cowardly attitude of hiding behind this fictitious show was revealed by a report in *Folha*, in which it was revealed that entire speeches by the character of the global pastor had been pilfered from an interview of Bishop Edir Macedo from *Veja* magazine. Another good moment of the newspaper was its special report "Holy War", a serious attempt at shedding more light than heat on the debate.

The Universal Church is an irritant only because of its visible growth and because of its links to a TV station. If it were not for its effectiveness to satisfy a demand that flabby Catholicism ignores, the Cardinal of Rio wouldn't be bothered..."

Part of this article reminds me of one serious journalist amid a wave of biased coverage. Octávio Frias de Oliveira, owner of the newspaper Folha de S. Paulo, always treated me with dignity. Not that he agreed with my convictions of faith, but he always respected me and understood the profound role of the Universal Church in helping people on the fringe of society; he said that to me in a meeting at the headquarters of Grupo Folha, in a spacious meeting room on Barão de Limeira Road, downtown São Paulo. Before giving me a hug of mutual support, he said he believed in the seriousness of the work of the Universal Church. His death has been a loss for Brazil.

A TUMOR

Overnight, Globo Network gave birth to an evangelical pastor who was also defender of its investments. In every report against the Universal Church or me, he would quickly appear on the air with a new scathing declaration. He was Reverend Caio Fábio D'Araújo Filho, connected to a traditional denomination at that time.

The goal was to try and add legitimacy to that station's attacks, using what was supposed to be a respected evangelical leader. For this reason, the reverend even assumed the post of president of the Brazilian Evangelical Association, founded with the intention of authenticating his position as leader. However, the organization had almost no representation.

In his television interviews, the reverend even ridiculed the sanctity of tithes and offerings, saying that the Universal Church made use of the tactic of "offering bags"—as if evangelical, Catholic, Orthodox, or spiritualist institutions had never used a bag to collect donations before.

In his most offen s ive and irresponsible statement, he claimed that the Universal Church was a "tumor" among the churches in Brazil.

You will discover what happened to him in a few pages.

CALCULATED REVENGE

Throughout the long course of the church's expansion, it has been common for pastors and bishops to leave. Many give up their service to God on the altar for a different way of life, and leave peacefully. But there is a particular group of men and women who upon leaving, attack us in a cowardly and deceitful manner. Ingratitude can be heard in their words of slander.

Many even pose as poor helpless victims and defenders of morality, at times on television, but hide their true faces. Anyone who has been removed from the Church was removed because of serious misconduct—some from unethical behavior of the most unimaginable and outrageous.

One attack, Christmas Eve 1995, was used by Globo to deliver one more blow to the Universal Church and to me. For days, images were shown of me happily counting donations of the church in Manhattan, New York. Other images of me relaxing with other bishops in a hotel in Jerusalem and Rio de Janeiro were shown out of context and with a criminal slant. This story and its impact occupied huge amounts of time over the course of several weeks on the station's main news show.

It was an act of revenge.

Days later I was told about a surprisingly aggressive statement of the former chief of Federal Police, Romeu Tuma—at that time a senator—published in the newspaper *O Estado de S. Paulo*, on December 28, 1995: "Interpol should investigate Universal," says Tuma.

The accusations trickled out, little by little. The main one turned into a fiasco. There was evidence of manipulation. Globo had made it seem like one-dollar bills, given as offering, were hundred-dollar bills. The thought-provoking program "25ª Hora" ("25th Hour"—an edgy, late night, commentary-debate program on current events), which was aired on Record, brought on experts that proved that the video had been unscrupulously edited.

Globo Network was forced to admit their wrongdoing on national television.

Shameful.

The adulteration of information and the Machiavellian exaggerations of this case caused protests at other media outlets.

I decided it was time to defend myself. We were fed up

with the countless low blows. I instructed "25ª Hora" to air a series of reports and debates informing Brazilians of the true story of Globo and its rotten practices. After airing for a few weeks, new allegations kept emerging—telephone recordings, videos from directors, documents. The viewing audience shot up. We started to have double-digit ratings during our late-night time slot.

More recently, in 2009, Globo Network attacked me and the Church again, using the same strategy and the same old accusations. I woke in the early morning hours in Portugal, and thought of a way to show Brazil the truth about this broadcaster. And so the historic edition of the newspaper *Folha Universal*, of September 26, 2009, came about. The entire paper was devoted to exposing the harm that the Rio--based broadcaster had done to the country.

The special edition, "How the Marinho family destroys Brazil", among other provocative topics, revealed the hidden story of the organization and its links with the previous military dictatorship, its links to the Time-Life scandal, its silence over the *"Diretas Já"* movement, loans that were suspected of being public money, the falsification of documents in the purchase of its São Paulo headquarters, and even illegal occupation of public land. The cover had a photo of the three brothers and heirs, the current owners.

Three and a half million copies of the special edition paper were printed in a single week. It was distributed by hand, to every office of the Executive, Legislative and Judiciary branches of the government, and interestingly enough, it was received very well.

Back in 1995, I recorded a radio program with a specific message about a painful moment that we lived through. I have selected an excerpt from my criticism, which incidentally fits perfectly with what is going on today:

"The malicious images shown by Globo are intended to tarnish the image of the Universal Church.

And yet we, the Universal Church, have never allowed ourselves to feel intimidated. We are not intimidated by an armed Goliath standing in front of us, because God is with us. And if God is for us, who can be against us? If God is for us, who can be our opponent, our enemy?

The devil is trying to destroy the Universal Church, the family of God, sealed by God, raised up by the Spirit of God. Who can destroy it?

Those who try are not fighting against a man, against Bishop Macedo, against the pastors. They are fighting against God.

Man did not give birth to the Universal Church. God gave birth to it. The people follow the Lord Jesus, not pastors, not me.

I ask: What has the Globo Network given you? What benefit has it had on your life? How about the Universal Church? What benefit has it had? Compare the two and come up with your own answer.

I challenge you who are not members of the Universal Church to put Globo Network to the side and attend the Universal Church for just one month and see what God will do in your life."

In February 2013, a similar article had a broader approach, with rhetorical arguments about the hostile climate caused by Globo Network. Below are some excerpts from this analysis:

Em Tempo newspaper

Edir Macedo, the man who transformed Brazil

"The man of greatest influence (and still far from being exhausted) in Brazil, in the second half of the 20th century, is Edir Macedo. Within a few decades, the country ceased to be overwhelmingly Catholic, and those who call themselves evangelicals now comprise the majority. In the wake of the Universal Church, others have come in waves…

In simple terms, the Catholic Church, on one hand, created a vacuum by giving unconvincing answers to certain questions like divorce, the pill, sex for procreation only, etc. Vicente Celestino celebrated the church with the song "Open Door"—rare these days—where there is always a trained assistant ready to listen to the down-and-out…

Understandably, opinions about Mr. Edir Macedo are passionate (for or against). But for having radically altered the religious character of the country, with all its implications, a calm, historical study is needed for him to be better understood by the Brazilian people. The transformation process will probably continue for another two or three decades. Why was tithing so important? With respect to the Trinity, why has worship focused so much on Jesus? The answers should be sociological rather than theological…

The gospel music "Festival Promessa" ("Promise Festival") in 2012, with artists from the record label branch of the broadcaster [Globo Network], was proof of the force unleashed by Mr. Edir Macedo."

There are two points and a question to be considered after this list of facts.

I chose to limit myself to the use of 1995 as a symbolic period to demonstrate the amount of manipulation that has been applied to make me, along with the Universal Church, disappear. Putting it bluntly, the goal was annihilation. The second relevant fact is that the audience of that station, at that time, was virtually absolute and reached 95% of Brazilian households at certain times of the day. In other words, without exaggeration, we were cruelly attacked by a weapon of mass destruction.

The question is plain and simple: Who could survive a "massacre" of that size? What man or institution could survive such a massive, violent wave of attacks?

The scars are here… exposed.

Almost 20 years later, I am filled with joy. Not because I have survived, but because of a certainty that the words of the Lord Jesus will be fulfilled:

"Blessed are you when they revile and persecute you, and say all kinds of evil against you falsely for My sake. Rejoice and be exceedingly glad, for great is your reward in heaven, for so they persecuted the prophets who were before you." (Matthew 5:11-12)

I share this joy with all the people of the church, who along with me, suffered with every sneer, every humiliation, every unjust attack, and who continue to be unshaken on the path of faith.

The reward in heaven is a reality.

LORD OF REASON

Today, after much time has passed, I cannot help but meditate on everything that happened and take stock of those events, examining my actions in light of our beliefs. The events of 1992, 1995 and other periods of our painful journey taught us lessons of the utmost importance.

The largest of them, perhaps, was a deeper understanding that we are nothing without God, as we will discuss in the coming chapter. Another lesson was to find strength where there was none, to pray for each one of the people that tried to harm us. I confess it was not a simple task, but I prayed to my God for everyone of them, no matter who they were.

Unfortunately, the lead characters of those years had different fates.

Fernando Collor de Mello was stripped of the Presidency of the Republic through impeachment.

PC Farias was found dead with his mistress in his beach house in Alagoas.

The businessman Jose Carlos Martinez died in a plane crash.

Leopoldo Collor died of throat cancer.

Judge João Carlos da Rocha Mattos was convicted of accepting bribes, spent eight years in prison and was barred from the bench.

Author Dias Gomes lost his life in a tragic car accident.

Former congressman Afanásio Jazadi has been forgotten. In his last election in 2008, he could not even be elected to the city council in São Paulo. His attempts to return to television have been unsuccessful.

Former senator Romeu Tuma died of multiple organ failure.

Former reverend Caio Fábio was involved in political scandals and lost his position in his church after making his extramarital relationship with his secretary public.

Jornal do Brazil went bankrupt and only exists on the Internet.

TV Manchete also went bankrupt and became extinct.

TV Globo has suffered repeated declines in recent decades and now has the worst audience ratings in its history.

MY GREATEST STRENGTH

Reliving the unfortunate past is painful. I do not hold grudges towards any person or institution, but have vivid memories of this time of great suffering. I look forward, as I always say. But the lessons have stuck, and have created an even greater responsibility for me to carry these days.

The Universal Church has advanced like never before. Millions of people spread through most of the countries of the world are under our spiritual direction. We run one of the largest media groups in Brazil and worldwide, which fights for a better, fairer, less monopolized society—to get rid of the Brazil we no longer want.

I depend on God for everything. He was with me in the most lonely and distressing moments, even though I was undeserving. Every morning, I recognize that I am not in the least worthy to lift my face to God. Who are the people of the Universal Church and who am I to ask for His help? We are less than nothing. But we are motivated by a deep, genuine sincerity, a faith that goes to the ends of the earth to achieve the impossible.

Whenever we think the end has come, God rises up to rescue us. In situations big and small, when we face a multitude of challenges in our own personal worlds, we can feel trapped. But that is our chance. We have to look to God. He is ready to listen to us at that very moment. He is eagerly waiting.

I survived, and you will too.

This is our life, and that of the Universal Church: complete dependence on God. We have established a solid, credible project in Brazil and in the world, but there is still much to do. Countless people who are lost continue to wait for our outstretched hand.

I remember some months ago, when I asked the bishops of Africa to spread the Gospel to the isolated villages of that continent, the response was immediate. Scenes of these missionary advances touched my heart and proved that there continues to be an endless mass of people thirsty for God.

Mumuila tribal villages, native communities in the desert, were among the first to accept us. These tribes live far away from everything, in one of the driest deserts in the world, in southern Angola. The region suffers from a lack of food, water and the basic necessities of life. Poverty forces many of their children to give up their childhood in order to work.

Over the last several decades, dozens of missionaries tried and failed to make inroads with this tribe. The locals continually rejected them, but now the Universal Church has been accepted. It is an outdoor church. The wooden benches are made from trees cut from the forest, and were made by the tribesmen themselves. As of this writing, there are no empty seats at the three meetings per week that we make for the Mumuila.

As I watched the images of our pastors in these distant, poor villages, I was moved to tears. Those threadbare, humble people are richer than many grand people living in big cities for one simple reason: they are so immersed in suffering that in the blink of an eye they surrender to the Lord Jesus and gain the most valuable thing a person can own.

This is the mission of the Universal Church. The same Spirit of the funeral parlor is still present today, in the primitive villages of Africa.

Scenes of desert-dwellers seeking God in an makeshift church without chairs, sound system, microphone, air conditioner, or even a roof, fills me with fear. This demands that we value our comfortable neighborhood church a few blocks away, or the small, simple church with few resources, and the altar that is accessible to the lost.

This forces us to reflect on the value of the church in our daily lives. The people of another country in Africa went through the brief but drama-filled experience of having their government close the doors of the church. Imagine waking up one day and finding that you no longer have a church near your home. Has that thought ever occurred to you? What would it be like to look for a house of God and not find one? Where would you go to renew your faith?

Where would you find comfort from the hardships of life? Where would you be challenged to exercise your faith and avoid losing your salvation?

This is the main reason for God's protection of the Universal Church and of me: we are obsessed with ending the hunger of the hungry… those hungry for the Word of God.

I will soon turn 70. I have every right to retire, to rest my weary body—my physical strength is not the same as when I was young. I could get a house by a lake, with a fishing boat, or live on a mountainside with trees and animals all around. I could spend the remaining years of my life traveling with Ester, enjoying the happiest phase of my marriage.

But I say no. We do the exact opposite. At this very moment, at this age, I shoulder a greater number of spiritual responsibilities. I spend my days preaching in the church or teaching our pastors and bishops around the world. And it will be like this until my last breath of life.

Why? I own nothing. My life is on the altar.

If I die today, all my personal property will be automatically donated to the Church. I made out my will in the United States. My children will inherit nothing, absolutely nothing, only the faith that leads us to a covenant with God.

A spiritual dream that came to me shortly before writing this book may best explain my idealism. The thought was that I had died and the angels carried me to the side of the Lord Jesus, and He then said to me:

"You could have done more. You could have won more souls."

This vision continually bothers me.

While I am alive, I need to give all I can for this conviction, to do all I can to snatch people from hell. I admit, this is a tough challenge. Most people forget that sooner or later, without the power to take anything with them, they will go straight to the cemetery. Their souls will be the only thing left. But where will it go? This makes me shudder in pain.

On my last visit to the construction site of the Temple of Solomon in March 2013, with half of the project complete, I placed my feet on the altar of our future church for the first time. I saw what the view would be from that hallowed ground.

For a few minutes, I slowly walked from side to side in silence.

I saw myself in the pavilion. I saw myself in the first meeting in the funeral parlor.

I saw myself as a young man seeking the Lord with a thirsty soul.

I saw myself alone, fighting against my own self in search of the Holy Spirit—the hours of crying out in search of the God of my life.

I saw myself fighting against the defeatism of evangelical leaders. The vote of confidence from my mother, the guarantor of the first Universal Church.

I saw myself in Maracanã in front of 200,000 people, the multiplying churches.

I saw myself in the firestorm of harsh, cruel attacks. The insults. The ridicule. The dishonor.

I saw myself going against my own desires and offering everything in sacrifice.

I saw God Himself. A man cannot do all this.

I saw my insignificance.

The construction of the Temple of Solomon makes my faith beat stronger. Each column, each pillar, each brick, each stone represents holiness. A place of grandeur, open to all people, of all religions. It is like a holy pregnancy: I can already see the Temple being born for the glory of God. The countdown coming to an end.

The project is unequalled, there is no precedent for it anywhere in the world. We have shed sweat and tears to erect this sacred building, millions in resources to care for thousands of people coming from all parts of the world. A historic achievement.

But thoughts about the Temple of Solomon, opening with all its splendor and beauty, does not fill me with as much joy as knowing that inside that building, someone, a single person, will have a genuine encounter with the God whom I have preached for more than 45 years.

My greatest dream will have come true. Lives surrendered on the altar.

The salvation of souls.

"NO WEAPON FORMED AGAINST YOU
SHALL PROSPER."

(Isaiah 54:17)